RACE AGAINST DEATH

THE GREATEST POW RESCUE
OF WORLD WAR II

ALSO BY
DEBORAH HOPKINSON

Giving a sick man a drink at the Cabanatuan prison camp on Luzon Island in the Philippines. Drawn from memory by artist Ben Steele, a prisoner of war in the Philippines and Japan during World War II.

RACE AGAINST DEATH

THE GREATEST POW RESCUE OF WORLD WAR II

BY

DEBORAH HOPKINSON

SCHOLASTIC
FOCUS
NEW YORK

Library of Congress Cataloging-in-Publication Data

Names: Hopkinson, Deborah, author.

Title: Race against death: the greatest POW rescue of World War II / by Deborah Hopkinson.

Description: New York : Scholastic Focus, [2023] | Includes bibliographical references and index. | Audience: Ages 9-12 | Audience: Grades 4-6 | Summary: "A thrilling account of the most daring American POW rescue mission of World War II. Following the bombing of Pearl Harbor, America entered World War II, and a new theater of battle opened up in the Pacific. But US troops, along with thousands of Filipino soldiers who fought alongside them, were overtaken in the Philippines by a fiercely determined Japanese navy, and many Americans and Filipino fighters were killed or captured. These American and Filipino prisoners of war were forced to endure the most horrific conditions on the deadly trek known as the Bataan Death March. Then, the American servicemen who were held captive by the Japanese military in Cabanatuan Camp and others in the Philippines, faced beatings, starvation, and tropical diseases, and lived constantly under the threat of death. Unable to forget their comrades' fate and concerned that these POWs would be brutally murdered as the tides of war shifted in the Pacific, the US Army Rangers undertook one of the most daring and dangerous rescue missions of all time. Aided by the "Angels of the Underground," the Sixth Ranger Battalion and courageous Filipino guerrilla soldiers set out on an uncertain and treacherous assignment. Often called the Great Raid, this remarkable story remains largely forgotten. Sibert Honor author Deborah Hopkinson presents an extraordinary and unflinching look at the heroic servicemen and women who courageously weathered the worst of circumstances and conditions in service to their country, as well as those who answered the call to save their fellow soldiers"— Provided by publisher.

Identifiers: LCCN 2022016416 | ISBN 9781338746167 (hardcover) | ISBN 9781338746174 (ebook)

Subjects: LCSH: United States. Army. Ranger Battalion, 6th—History—Juvenile literature. | World War, 1939-1945—Campaigns—Philippines—Cabanatuan— Juvenile literature. | World War, 1939-1945—Concentration camps— Philippines—Cabanatuan—Juvenile literature. | World War, 1939-1945— Prisoners and prisons, Japanese—Juvenile literature. | BISAC: JUVENILE NONFICTION / History / Military & Wars | JUVENILE NONFICTION / History / Holocaust

Classification: LCC D767.4 .H67 2023 | DDC 940.54/7252095991—dc23/eng/20220406

LC record available at https://lccn.loc.gov/2022016416

10 9 8 7 6 5 4 3 2 1   23 24 25 26 27

Printed in Italy   183

First edition, April 2023

Book design by Keirsten Geise

*For all who have served and suffered
in conflicts, then and now*

And for the people of Ukraine

—DH

"Please let others read this story lest we forget."

—James "Hank" Cowan, liberated
POW of Cabanatuan

"The bravest are usually those whom
we do not know or hear about . . ."

—F. Sionil José, Filipino author

BEFORE YOU BEGIN

This is the story of the greatest POW rescue of World War II. It took place on January 30, 1945, when more than five hundred prisoners of war (POWs) were freed in a daring raid on Cabanatuan [cabana tú ahn] prison camp in the Philippines. Most were American soldiers who'd survived the Bataan Death March in 1942 and nearly three subsequent years of imprisonment under brutal conditions.

A movie about the rescue called *The Great Raid* came out in 2005. But the true story is much more than a war action film. Because to know what liberation meant to the POWs, we must understand how they got there, what they endured, and how many had already been lost. To know why the perilous rescue was a race against death, we must realize what was about to happen if it didn't take place.

Although World War II had been raging in Europe since September 1939, the United States of America didn't enter it until Japan attacked Pearl Harbor in December 1941.

That's when a young soldier named James Henry Cowan begins our story. His friends and family called him Hank, so we will too.

BUZZING ENGINES
IN THE SKY

Place: *Clark Field, American air base in the Philippines*
Date: *Monday, December 8, in the Philippines (still December 7 in Hawai'i)*
Time: *Ten hours after the Pearl Harbor attack*

"I had been working on an engine on one of our B-17s in the morning and had just returned from lunch," said Private James Henry "Hank" Cowan. "I had barely started when I heard the sound of many airplanes."

Hank was a young aircraft mechanic stationed at Clark Field, a major American air base about forty-five miles from the capital city of Manila on Luzon Island in the Philippines. The seventh of eight children, Hank was the first in his family to graduate from high school. During the Great Depression, Hank had worked in the Civilian Conservation Corps before joining the U.S. Army Air Corps and being sent to the Philippines.

Hank was proud of the giant, four-engine B-17s he cared for at Clark Field. In his eyes, these magnificent planes were "some of the finest in the world."

It was a little after noon on Monday, December 8, 1941, Philippine time. But in Hawai'i, it was still Sunday evening on a day Americans would never forget. Like everyone else, Hank was reeling from the news of Japan's surprise attack on

The battleship USS *California* after the attack on Pearl Harbor on Sunday morning, December 7, 1941, Hawai'i time.

US battleships at the US Navy base at Pearl Harbor, just ten hours before.

In Manila, General Douglas MacArthur, commander of the US Army Forces in the Far East, had been alerted to the Pearl Harbor assault by phone in the early hours of December 8. (The Philippines is eighteen hours ahead of Hawai'i. So it was 2:00 a.m. Monday morning in Manila when the attack took place.)

That time difference meant that people in the Philippines found out about Pearl Harbor on Monday morning when they turned on radios or opened their newspapers. Everyone, Filipino and American alike, knew what it meant: America was now thrust into war with Japan and its Axis allies, Italy and Nazi Germany. Everyone knew something else too: The Philippines was sure to be one of Japan's next targets.

Japan lay nearly two thousand miles north of the Philippine Islands, an archipelago of more than seven thousand islands. (Luzon, where our story takes place, is the largest and most populous island.) Though Japan itself was distant, the Japanese also maintained air bases on Formosa (now Taiwan), about seven hundred miles away—within striking distance by air.

Hank and other American soldiers stationed in the Philippines anticipated that American planes would be ordered to attack Formosa first thing Monday morning. Yet, for some unexplained reason, the order didn't come right away. (Historians still debate the details.) Instead, some of the B-17 bombers at Clark were sent to patrol the skies above Luzon on a reconnaissance mission.

Finally, at about 11:00 a.m., the B-17s were ordered back to base. The bureaucratic knot had been untangled and a retaliatory strike on Formosa was a go. Now the ground crew could scramble to load the powerful bombers with fuel and ammunition for the mission.

That's when Hank heard the buzz of engines overhead.

"I looked up to see a tremendous formation. They were at high altitude in perfect formation against the blue Philippine sky," he said. "I started counting and someone said, 'Oh look at the beautiful Navy formation.' By then I had counted 54. Then all of a sudden I realized what was happening.

"I yelled, 'Navy, Hell!'"

RACE AGAINST DEATH

THE GREATEST POW RESCUE OF WORLD WAR II

CONTENTS

PART 1 FROM SHOCK TO SURRENDER
December 1941–Spring 1942

PART 2 ENDURANCE AND RESISTANCE
Spring 1942–Fall 1944

PART 3 RACE AGAINST DEATH

Fall 1944–Winter 1945

ABOUT THE PEOPLE
IN THIS BOOK

Many voices contribute to this story, which takes place over more than three years. We'll follow a few people from 1941 to the 1945 rescue, while others pass in and out. To aid readers, in addition to the list below, I've included the names of main eyewitnesses at the start of each chapter.

Books about the past like this one are only possible thanks to the courage of people who've told their stories in oral histories, memoirs sometimes long out of print, or in magazine articles and interviews. Without such testimony, much of history is lost.

I'm immensely grateful to the POW survivors who shared memories, often searing and painful; and to the volunteers and archivists in museums, universities, and libraries who have preserved their testimonies. Special thanks go to family members who provided photos, especially Carolyn Mangler, daughter of James "Hank" Cowan, for sharing photographs and anecdotes and helping her dad create a record of his war experiences. Learning more about Hank through his family is a reminder of how vital it is to capture our own stories—and those of people we love.

So tell your story. Don't let your history vanish.

LORENZO Y. BANEGAS (1919–2001) was born in New Mexico and was one of about eighteen hundred New Mexico National Guard soldiers sent to the Philippines in September 1941 as part of the 200th Coast Artillery. He survived the Bataan Death March, and was a POW at Cabanatuan and in Japan. He was known for cheering up other patients in "Zero Ward" at Cabanatuan. His oral history interview is part of the Veterans History Project of the Library of Congress.

PILAR CAMPOS (circa 1917–1945) was a young Filipina woman who had attended college in the United States before returning to Manila. During the Japanese occupation, she became active in the Philippine underground, bringing food and medicine to her then-boyfriend, American POW Dr. Ralph Hibbs, and other prisoners. Nicknamed "Petie," she was brutally murdered by Japanese military police because of her underground activities.

JAMES HENRY "HANK" COWAN (1920–1988) was a soldier stationed at Clark Field and later in Bataan who survived the Bataan Death March and spent nearly three years in Cabanatuan prison camp. Hank was originally an airplane mechanic, but after planes were destroyed in the attack on Clark Field, he was ordered into an antiaircraft unit, the 200th Coast Artillery (the same unit to which Lorenzo Banegas and Ruben Flores belonged). He returned to the United States and met his wife, Ginny, on a blind date soon after coming home. They married in 1945 and had three children. They loved camping, square dancing, and traveling.

WILLIAM "ED" DYESS (1916–1943) was an army pilot at Clark Field who survived the Bataan Death March and escaped from the Philippines, returning to the United States in July 1943. His firsthand account of the atrocities committed against Allied soldiers during the Bataan Death March shocked the American public when it was published in 1944. Ed was killed in a training accident on December 22, 1943, at age twenty-seven.

RUBEN FLORES (1917–2002) was born in Las Cruces, New Mexico, and joined the merchant marines. He was inducted into the army in April 1941 and was deployed to the Philippines that same year, becoming part of the 200th Coast Artillery. He survived the Bataan Death March, Cabanatuan, and prison camps in Japan. He later was a member of the Las Cruces Chapter of the Bataan Veterans Organization.

SAMUEL C. GRASHIO (1918–1999) was a fighter pilot under the command of squadron leader Ed Dyess. Sam and Ed were part of a group of prisoners who escaped from a prison camp on Mindanao Island and brought home eyewitness reports of the Bataan Death March and conditions in POW camps.

RALPH E. HIBBS (1913–2000) was a battalion surgeon in the Thirty-First Infantry Regiment who survived the Bataan Death March and was liberated from Cabanatuan, where he treated patients in the tuberculosis ward. He wrote a book about his ordeal and later helped to arrange official recognition of the bravery of underground activist Pilar Campos, his girlfriend in Manila. He had a successful postwar career as a physician in Oregon.

WALTER KRUEGER (1881–1967) was the general in charge of the Sixth Army who authorized the POW rescue mission on Cabanatuan in January 1945.

ROBERT LAPHAM (1917–2003) was an army officer who escaped capture on Bataan and went on to command the Luzon Guerrilla Armed Forces (LGAF) or "Lapham's Raiders," an army of thirteen thousand Filipino guerrilla fighters behind Japanese lines.

HENRY G. LEE (1914–1945), a survivor of the Bataan Death March, was imprisoned at Cabanatuan when he began writing poetry. He buried his notebooks under his barrack when he was transported to Japan in December 1944. He was killed along with other American POWs on the Japanese ship *Enoura Maru* when it was attacked by US planes in January 1945.

DOUGLAS MACARTHUR (1880–1964) was the major general in charge of US Forces in the Far East. Stationed in Manila when the war broke out, he was forced to leave the Philippines when ordered by President Franklin D. Roosevelt to evacuate to Australia in March 1942. From there, he commanded military operations in the southwest Pacific, leading the US assault against Japan. He made a triumphant return to the Philippines in the fall of 1944 and later administered the Allied postwar occupation of Japan.

HENRY MUCCI (1909–1997) was an army colonel and commander of the Sixth Rangers, a unit specializing in commando-type operations. He planned and led the Cabanatuan rescue mission and became a popular war hero.

CARL MYDANS (1907–2004) was a photographer for *Life* magazine. While on assignment in the Philippines, he and his journalist wife, Shelly Smith Mydans (1938–2002), were captured and held in prison facilities on the campus of Santo Tomas University in Manila. They were later moved to Shanghai and released on a prisoner exchange program. Carl returned to the Philippines along with US troops in the fall of 1944.

JUAN PAJOTA (1914–1976) was a Filipino guerrilla captain working with Robert Lapham's group and is recognized as one of the heroes in the successful Cabanatuan POW rescue. He died in the United States while in the process of becoming an American citizen.

ROBERT PRINCE (1919–2009), originally from Washington State, graduated from Stanford University in 1941. He trained as a Ranger in New Guinea, landed on Luzon Island in January 1945, and, under Henry Mucci, helped plan and lead the Cabanatuan rescue mission.

MANUEL QUEZON (1878–1944) was president of the Philippines from 1935 until his death. He headed the government as it transitioned from a territory of the United States to becoming an independent nation. He died in exile in the United States after being evacuated from Corregidor following the Japanese occupation in early 1942.

CARLOS P. ROMULO (1899–1985) was a Filipino journalist and member of General Douglas MacArthur's staff who escaped from Corregidor and Bataan in April 1942. He later held prominent positions in the Philippines and was the first Asian to become president of the United Nations General Assembly.

AMEA BREWIN WILLOUGHBY (1909–1970) was an American who moved to the Philippines in 1939 with her husband, Woodbury "Woody" Willoughby, a US diplomat charged with saving the gold of the treasury of the Philippines.

LUCY WILSON (later Jopling) (1916–2000) was an army nurse evacuated to Bataan and Corregidor who escaped on one of the last submarines to leave the Philippines. She later returned to the Pacific to help evacuate wounded soldiers from battlefields. Lucy married Dan Jopling, a former POW, and they became the parents of four children. Her remarkable memoir of her life is entitled *Warrior in White*.

A SPECIAL NOTE FROM THE AUTHOR

All authors face choices when telling complex true stories from history, and no one book can convey everything. So before we go on, I want to say a little about the scope of this book.

Many of the voices here have been natural choices: They belong to people who lived through these events and left behind a compelling memoir or oral history. But, of course, they are just a few of the many thousands involved in World War II in the Philippines. This book focuses primarily on American soldiers; the stories of individual Filipinos are best told by others.

Also, *Race Against Death* was written as an introduction rather than an in-depth military history or a detailed analysis of the Cabanatuan raid itself. Want to learn more? Check out the bibliography and online links in the back.

You may also want to know that most of the American soldiers in the story are white, as were most American soldiers in the early days of the war in the Philippines. I found oral history interviews with several Latino soldiers who survived the Bataan Death March. These young men were part of the 200th Coast Artillery Regiment, activated from the New Mexico National Guard, and arrived in the Philippines in the fall of 1941. You'll meet a couple of them here, and I've included online links to so you can see photos and watch oral history videos.

During World War II, women didn't hold combat roles, though dozens of female military nurses served on Bataan. The nurses became the largest group of American women to be held as POWs in World War II when they were interned with civilian prisoners on the grounds of Santo Tomas University in Manila and liberated in 1945.

African American men did fight in the Pacific, serving in segregated units activated later in the war. However, from the outset, Black American sailors were essential crew members on navy ships and submarines, although racism relegated them to non-combat positions as stewards and cooks. Combat was a different story. Navy cook Dorie Miller became the first Black American awarded the Navy Cross for his heroic actions at Pearl Harbor. During battle stations, Black submariners like steward Walter Pye Wilson on the USS *Trigger* was relied on to steer the ship. (You can read more about him in my book *Dive!*)

Finally, a word about language and atrocities committed against POWs. Japan is now a close ally of the United States, but was a sworn enemy during World War II. Racial slurs we consider harmful and pejorative are found both in individual soldiers' and even in official military reports. I have avoided these as unnecessary.

Nonetheless, the barbaric treatment of POWs by Japanese guards is well-documented; it led to higher death rates of prisoners of war in the Philippines than in any other theater of the war. These instances are difficult to read about, and there are several here that may be disturbing to some readers.

After the war, former POWs testified at the Tokyo War Crimes trials, leading to the conviction of Japanese military leaders, but many individual guards and soldiers guilty of the worst atrocities had been killed or were never identified.

On the home front, the war against Japan led to racial hatred, extreme anti-Japanese prejudice, and the forced relocation and incarceration of thousands of innocent Japanese American families in internment camps. That, too, is beyond the scope of this story.

Unfortunately, since I wrote this book during a time when international travel wasn't possible, I wasn't able to visit the Philippines. We've included many photos, though, which help us see what this time in history was like.

I've written other books about World War II, but while researching this one I realized how little I knew about the war in the Philippines, the Bataan Death March, and the heartbreaking experiences of American prisoners of war. I hope reading *Race Against Death* encourages you to reflect on the lives of these courageous individuals and continue to learn about the past and our world.

The events you will read about here may seem like something from a far distant past. But just as we were finalizing this book for publication, an unjust, unjustified war began, when Russia invaded Ukraine in February 2022. Once again, innocent children are suffering and the lives and homes of families are shattered. Once again, we witness the extraordinary courage of ordinary people engaged in resistance against tyranny.

I cannot know what the world will be like when you pick up this book. But I thank you for choosing to open your heart to these stories and those who struggled, as we must still do, to create a world that respects individual rights and democratic ideals.

Deborah Hopkinson
March 2022

Three stricken US battleships after the December 7, 1941, attack on Pearl Harbor. From left to right: USS *West Virginia* (severely damaged), USS *Tennessee* (damaged), and the USS *Arizona* (sunk).

PART 1

FROM SHOCK TO SURRENDER

December 1941–Spring 1942

"To the Congress of the United States: Yesterday, December 7, 1941— a date which will live in infamy—the United States of America was suddenly and deliberately attacked by naval and air forces of the Empire of Japan . . ."

—President Franklin D. Roosevelt
Joint Address to Congress Leading to a
Declaration of War against Japan
December 8, 1941

"*The military unpreparedness of the United States in the Pacific in 1941 can only be called appalling.*"

—Robert Lapham
American guerrilla leader
in the Philippines

The remains of the USS *Arizona* in Pearl Harbor on December 10, 1941.

CHAPTER 1

THE FIRST DAYS: HORROR AND DESTRUCTION

EYEWITNESSES: HANK COWAN, SAM GRASHIO, LUCY WILSON, RALPH HIBBS

Day #1, December 8—Clark Field

One minute, Private Hank Cowan was coming back to work from lunch. The next, he was racing for shelter. The open spaces of Clark Field offered little protection. The best he could do was leap into a drainage ditch at the edge of the airfield. The ditch was soon crammed with other terrified soldiers.

Above them, wave after wave of Japanese planes descended out of a clear blue sky. The heavy bombers roared in first, followed by agile Zero fighter planes that strafed the field with machine gun fire. Japanese pilots later expressed surprise at seeing so many American planes lined up wing-to-wing like perfect targets—sitting ducks.

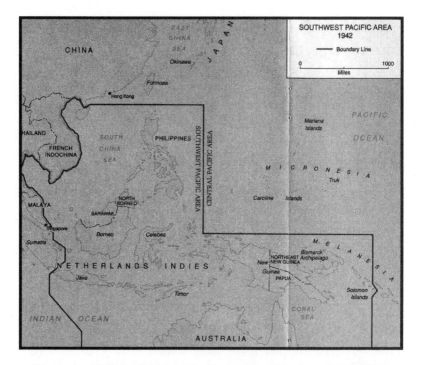

This map from 1942 shows the location of Formosa (now Taiwan), north of the Philippines. America's delay in launching an immediate counterattack against Japanese bases led to devastation at Clark Field.

"I snuggled as close to the side of the ditch as possible," said Hank. "If they [the attack planes] had come down the ditch they would have killed a lot of us."

The valuable bombers were the enemy's main targets, but even so, Hank was almost hit. "A burst of 20 mm fire knocked off the side of the ditch and partially covered me with dirt."

In an instant, Clark Field had gone from calm to chaos. "As the bombers passed over, the Americans could see the falling bombs glistening in the sunlight," wrote military historian Louis Morton. "Then came the explosions, hundreds of them, so violent that they seemed to pierce the eardrums and shake the ground . . .

"The scene was one of destruction and horror, unbelievable to the men who only a few minutes before had been eating lunch or servicing the planes . . . Dense smoke and a heavy cloud of dust rose over the field."

Hank had a front-row seat. "The Japanese did a thorough job of destroying our base," he reflected. "After the attack, our troops were scared and demoralized, as well as bewildered."

The destruction of American air power in the Philippines was the day's second Pearl Harbor. Only seventeen of the

James "Hank" Cowan began his war at Clark Field and would become a prisoner at Cabanatuan until liberated on January 30, 1945.

thirty-five powerful B-17 bombers were spared. More than seventy-five other planes were destroyed, including fifty-three P-40 fighter planes. The attack also brought a heavy human toll: Eighty people were killed and 150 wounded.

Clark Field marked the start of Hank Cowan's war. He couldn't know it then, but his ordeal in the Philippines would last for more than three years—most of it as a POW at Cabanatuan prison camp.

Other young soldiers were also thrust into sudden combat that day. One of them, a fighter pilot named Sam Grashio, was almost shot out of the sky on the first day of the war—right above Clark Field.

Sam Grashio had been obsessed with flying ever since he was a boy. Born in Spokane, Washington, Sam had joined the Washington National Guard in 1939 with a good friend. It seemed "the only way near-penniless youths like ourselves would ever actually get to fly."

Sam was commissioned as a second lieutenant in the Army Air Corps in April 1941; he arrived at his post at Nichols Field, the other major air base in the Philippines, on November 20, just days before war broke out.

During flight training, the prospect of war had seemed

Fighter pilot Sam Grashio.

far off. "I thought of flying only in the narrow sense: taking to the air in the best World War I movie tradition, embellished with goggles and helmet, scarf waving in the breeze," said Sam. "I thought little about why I was training and flying so much."

Even after arriving in the Philippines, Sam hadn't taken the rumblings of war too seriously. In fact, on December 6, he made a bet of five pesos with his squadron commander, Ed Dyess, that there would be no war with Japan. "Ed took the bet at once and laid another five that war would begin within a week," said Sam.

William E. "Ed" Dyess, captain of the Twenty-First Pursuit Squadron of the US Army Air Forces, was Sam's commander and friend. Ed had grown up in the small town of Albany, Texas. Like Sam, he'd fallen in love with aviation as a kid. After he graduated from college, he decided to become a pilot and joined the army in 1937.

Sam later wrote that Ed "was the most inspiring military officer I have ever known . . . He was impressive in bearing: tall, husky, with deep piercing blue eyes. He was intelligent, magnetic, and fearless: a natural leader who commanded respect without being intimidating. His pilots revered him and would have followed him anywhere."

Unlike Sam, before Ed had shipped out to the Philippines on November 1, he'd heard enough about tensions between the US and Japan to convince him war was inevitable. Not only that, he had "no doubt that Manila would be Japan's first target."

Ed had it right.

After the news of Pearl Harbor broke on Monday morning, Sam and other pilots were sent up from Nichols Field to try out their new P-40 single-seat fighter planes, firing their machine guns into a lake as target practice. The planes were so untested that a few developed technical problems, forcing pilots to return to base.

Fighter pilot and squadron leader Ed Dyess.

After target practice, Sam led three other pilots to check out the situation at Clark Field. At first, all appeared quiet: They saw nothing but peace and blue sky. But just as they were heading back to Nichols, a hysterical message from the tower operator at Clark came blasting into their headphones. Clark was being bombed—all P-40s should return to help.

"We turned back to Clark," said Sam. "In the distance I got my first glimpse of the spectacular destructiveness of war. It was astounding! Where the airfield should have been the whole area was boiling with smoke, dust, and flames."

Spotting enemy bombers, Sam ordered his group to attack. Suddenly, two Japanese Zero fighters closed in on him and opened fire.

"I veered sharply to the left. My plane shuddered as a burst hit the left wing, and blew a hole big enough to throw a hat through, as Ed Dyess put it later," said Sam. "For the first time that day I had the hell scared out of me. Momentarily, I was sure I was going to die on the first day of the war."

Recalling his training and the advice Ed had given him about dealing with a Zero, Sam didn't try to outpace the faster planes. Instead, he plunged into a deep dive. "The wind shrieked past me and the earth flashed upward at horrifying speed. According to the book, I was courting suicide," he said.

The manuals advised against a dive like this in a new, untested plane. Sam's P-40 had been in the air for a grand total of about two hours! But what choice did he have?

Sam's luck held and he made it back to Nichols. Later that day, Ed Dyess ordered the P-40s and their pilots to Clark Field to spend the night, on the assumption that the enemy wouldn't strike Clark again so soon. Ed wanted the planes away from Nichols Field: He figured it was likely next on the target list.

Once again, Ed was correct.

Day #2, December 9–Nichols Field

Lucy Wilson (later Lucy Wilson Jopling) worked the night shift at the military hospital at Fort McKinley, not far from Nichols Field.

Pearl Harbor had already turned her life upside down. As soon as the twenty-four-year-old army nurse from Texas had gotten off duty Monday morning, she'd been fitted with a helmet and gas mask—all to prepare for the air raids sure to come. Lucy didn't get a chance to sleep before going back on the ward Monday evening.

Army nurse Lucy Wilson Jopling.

She wouldn't get much rest that night either.

Nurses were allowed to nap in an empty room during the night if their wards weren't busy. Lucy made sure her patients were settled. Then in the early morning hours of Tuesday, December 9, she'd headed to the break room to grab some rest. "I had barely gotten to sleep when the loudest noise I had ever heard in my life began. I tore down the mosquito net getting out of bed. I was so scared I was nauseated."

She could guess what was happening: Nichols Field was under attack. "I kept looking at the ceiling and walls to see why they didn't come tumbling down," Lucy remembered. "After a few seconds I realized I would be receiving new patients and I had better get prepared."

Lucy sprang into action. She roused any patients well enough to stand and made them get out of bed to free up space. By the time she'd gathered morphine and other supplies, wounded men were being rushed in.

Lucy had no time for charts or paperwork: To keep track of those she'd treated, she simply drew an X mark on each patient's forehead after she'd given him one dose of morphine, a powerful painkiller.

Displaying the quick-thinking and battlefield nursing skills she would use throughout the war, Lucy had everything under control before doctors even got there. "I had a ward full of patients before they arrived—and began making decisions on who would go to surgery first."

On most mornings, Lieutenant Ralph Hibbs woke up in his off-base apartment and started his day with coffee and a newspaper. Originally from Iowa, the young battalion surgeon had been enjoying a relaxed peacetime lifestyle since arriving in the Philippines on June 20, 1941. So far, Ralph had only light duties as a junior officer with the Thirty-First US Infantry Regiment.

In fact, sharing an apartment in Manila with other physicians, Ralph had been able to play golf, enjoy nightclubs, and date twenty-four-year-old Pilar Campos, a young Manila woman who spoke five languages and had graduated from college in the United States.

The brave and vibrant Pilar Campos risked her life to bring food and medicine to American POWs—including her boyfriend, Dr. Ralph Hibbs.

(There are several languages spoken throughout the Philippines. In the 1930s, Tagalog [later also called Filipino] was selected as the national language; it is one of two official languages today, the other being English.) The daughter of a bank president, Pilar taught English at Philippine University and was the society editor for the newspaper *Manila Herald*.

At the end of November, as he and Pilar danced in the evenings, Ralph wrote his parents back home that an attack on the Philippines seemed unlikely. He was having fun, but as for action, this was the wrong place. "'If I had to do it over again, I would have gone to England,'" he told them. "'There's nothing going to happen here.'"

And then came December 8. On Monday morning, he'd opened his newspaper to the devastating headlines. "A sinking nausea gripped my midsection—a feeling that was to be repeated so often during combat."

Ralph made his way to his battalion headquarters at Nichols Field, where he was issued a pistol along with a shovel to dig his own foxhole for shelter. He slept on a cot in a tent on Monday night. That's when the scream of falling bombs exploding nearby startled him awake, just as it had frightened Lucy Wilson at the hospital not far away.

"The shrieking crescendo filled me with terror. My whole body shook. The explosions seemed not to crack my ears, but to shake my insides." Ralph dove out of his cot, making a hole in the mosquito netting. Outside the tent, men were frantically digging foxhole shelters in the earth.

"Damn it, in my panic, I couldn't find my shovel!"

. . .

At daylight, Ralph got his first look at the damage. "Nichols Field was in shambles, covered with greasy smoke, fires burning out of control and collapsed buildings. The planes on the ground, the barracks, fuel tanks, repair shops; all lay in complete ruin. The last major U.S. airfield was destroyed," he said.

"Obviously, we were going to have to fight the rest of the war without any significant air power." Ralph was right. In just a matter of days, Japan had decimated America's battleships and planes in the Pacific. But Japan's well-planned onslaught on American defenses in the Philippines wasn't over yet.

US Army Air Corps P-35s were attacked on Nichols Field on December 9 and 10, 1941.

Day #3, December 10—Cavite Naval Base

The start of the war also affected civilians in the Philippines, including Americans. One was Amea Brewin Willoughby, the young wife of a high-ranking US diplomat, who'd moved to Manila in 1939 with her husband, Woodbury "Woody" Willoughby.

As a diplomatic spouse, Amea didn't get paid (most still don't), but she was an active Red Cross hospital volunteer and kept busy with social duties. Woody was the second-in-command to High Commissioner Francis Sayre, who served as President Franklin D. Roosevelt's representative to the Philippine government.

Amea had been devastated by the surprise attack on Pearl Harbor. "The whole of my life had turned upside down," said Amea. "But, like so many other millions of Americans on that incredible day, I had no idea of the vastness of the change."

The shocks kept coming: Pearl Harbor, Clark, Nichols. Then, on December 10, Amea and Woody witnessed the destruction of Cavite Naval Base located on Manila Bay, one of the most strategic harbors in the Pacific. With American air support devastated, Cavite was an easy target for an enemy air attack.

Sitting on a seawall overlooking the bay, Amea saw the Japanese heavy bombers flying in a low V shape, almost like wild geese. They made straight for Cavite, about four miles away. No American planes rose to stop them.

Cavite Naval Base on fire. The loss of Cavite meant that the US submarine base in Asia was forced to relocate to Australia.

Amea saw "heavy masses of earth thrown into the air, pushing before them dense clouds of smoke and debris. Then, seconds later, the overlapping cacophony and thunder of the explosions came deafeningly across the water and grew into one long, uninterrupted roar of bombs.

"Would it never stop? Was there ever a time when there had been no shock of bombs, no trembling of the earth?"

Amea and Woody could only stare in horrified surprise. "It was sickening and frightening to know of the destruction of so much of the little strength that we had. But right before us we could see with our own eyes the ruin of one of America's greatest naval bases—and the only U.S. base in the Far East."

The war in the Pacific was just a few days old, yet Japan now had a tremendous tactical advantage. "Everywhere the

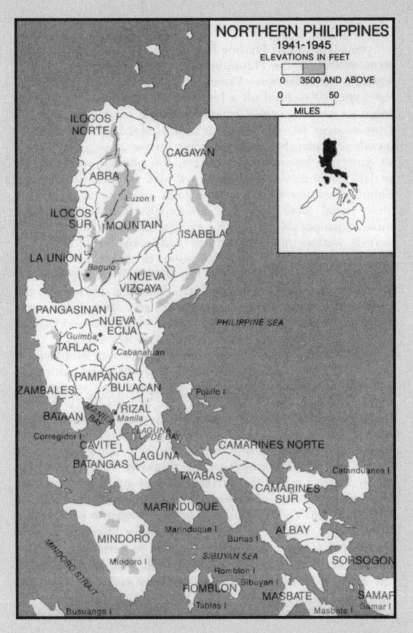

The map above shows the Northern Philippines, including the island of Luzon, while the one on the next page illustrates the coordinated Japanese strategy that led to rapid domination of the Pacific region in the early part of the war. That map and inset photo of a Japanese plane (Mitsubishi G3M bomber) are from a Japanese book from the time entitled *Photographic History of Naval Strategy*.

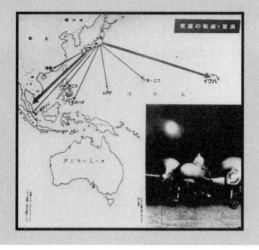

The Navy History and Heritage Command translated the caption from the original Japanese as: "This chart shows points attacked by our Navy Eagles, 8–10 December. Left to right: Hong Kong, Kota Bharu (Malaysia), Singapore, Manila [P.I.], Davao, Guam, Wake, Hawaii."

Allies seemed dazed at the tempo of Japanese operations," pilot Sam Grashio wrote later. "Each day seemed to bring news of some fresh disaster."

Along with Pearl Harbor and the Philippines, Japan had struck American and British bases in Guam, Wake Island, Midway Island, and Hong Kong. In the Philippines, with America's ability to defend the territory nearly crushed, Japan didn't wait long for the next stage: invasion.

Invasion had been part of the enemy's plan from the outset. Japan landed its first advance ground forces on December 8. On December 22, 1941, about forty-three thousand Japanese troops breached the shores of Lingayen Gulf on Luzon with orders to push south toward Manila. Any hope the Allies had of holding the beaches was, of course, now gone.

And so, as a delaying action until reinforcements could arrive, General Douglas MacArthur informed officials in Washington of his plan to withdraw all Philippine and American military forces to the peninsula of Bataan.

The Battle of Bataan was about to begin.

BEFORE WE HEAD TO BATAAN: A BIT OF BACKGROUND

The three-month siege known as the Battle of Bataan was one of the worst defeats in US military history. Yet it was also a remarkable feat of perseverance by young Filipino and American men. Many were recent recruits with little training; most were experiencing combat for the first time.

To understand why American diplomats and military were there in the first place, it's helpful to know a bit of history. The Philippines had been under the control of Spain since the sixteenth century. It became a territory of the United States in 1898 as a result of the Spanish-American War, which was fought in both the Caribbean and the Pacific.

After America defeated Spain, the US took over lands that had belonged to Spain, including Puerto Rico, Guam, and the Philippines. (Today, Puerto Rico and Guam remain US territories, where residents are US citizens but lack some of the benefits of citizenship, such as voting in national elections and having voting representatives in Congress.)

People in the Philippines had been pushing for independence from Spain, and continued their efforts when America gained control. The United States eventually agreed, and in 1934, Congress passed legislation that set in place a ten-year process for the Philippines to achieve full independence, which took place in 1946 (the war delayed it for two years).

During the transition period, the United States would be able to maintain military bases in the islands and call

Philippine military forces into service. To prepare for independence, the interim Commonwealth Government of the Philippines also wanted to expand its own army and defense capabilities. And for this Philippine president Manuel L. Quezon turned to an old friend: General Douglas MacArthur.

General Douglas MacArthur served as commander of the US Army Forces in the Far East (USAFFE).

Douglas MacArthur was born into a military family in Little Rock, Arkansas, and graduated from West Point in 1903. His father, also a well-known general, had served as governor general in the Philippines. MacArthur climbed the military ranks during World War I. In 1935, he became the chief military advisor to President Quezon.

MacArthur officially retired from the US Army in 1937, but was called back to active service in July 1941 and made commander of a new organizational entity, the US Army Forces in the Far East (USAFFE), with the rank of major general. He was then living in Manila with his wife, Jean, and their young son, Arthur, who was not quite four.

The timing of MacArthur's appointment was no accident. War clouds were gathering; international tensions had increased, and military planners in Washington wanted an experienced hand in this strategic territory in the Pacific.

At this time, the Philippine forces consisted of a little more than twenty-two thousand men, of whom nearly twelve thousand were Philippine Scouts, a military unit begun in 1901. The Philippine Scouts were trained Filipino soldiers who were part of the regular US Army thanks to the territorial status of the Philippines. Some notable Philippine Scouts such as Captain Juan Pajota (whom we'll meet in Part Three) became guerrilla fighters behind enemy lines after the Japanese invasion. Guerrilla warfare is an irregular type of combat conducted by small, mobile groups of fighters who launch small-scale operations such as ambushes, sabotage, or hit-and-run attacks.

But the Philippine Scouts represented only a small segment of the Filipino army. As tensions between Japan and the US intensified, MacArthur stepped up his recruitment efforts. On September 1, 1941, MacArthur began to mobilize Philippine army reserves, train more officers, and recruit more soldiers. The effort was barely underway when Japan attacked. The result was that many of the 120,000 soldiers in the Philippine Army (excepting the Philippine Scouts) were not well trained. Moreover, there was a shortage of vehicles and equipment.

Historian Louis Morton described the average uniform for the Philippine soldier as "shorts, short-sleeved shirt, and cheap canvas shoes with a rubber sole that wore out in about two weeks." One division had gas masks but no steel helmets.

. . .

Back in Washington, with the experienced MacArthur now in place, the US War Department also stepped up support. The department authorized additional tanks, antiaircraft artillery, planes, and personnel to increase defense capacity in the Philippines. This included the deployment of nurses like Lucy Wilson and the pilots and soldiers we've just met in this chapter.

It also encompassed activating the 200th Coast Artillery, an outgrowth of the New Mexico National Guard, whose members had been undergoing intensive artillery training in the United States before being tapped for overseas assignment. This deployment brought to the Philippines 76 officers and 1,681 enlisted men from New Mexico. The group included a number of Latino soldiers. Many of the soldiers were from small towns in the state and knew one another.

With nearly 1,800 men from New Mexico in the Philippines when war broke out, the state suffered terrible losses during the Bataan Death March and in prison camps. This connection between the state and the Philippines is honored to this day: Since 1989, New Mexico has commemorated those who suffered and died on the Death March with an annual marathon.

MacARTHUR'S DEFENSE PLAN, DECEMBER 1941

With the landing of Japanese ground forces imminent, MacArthur decided to move his forces away from Manila and make a stand on the Bataan Peninsula; he'd received approval for his overall defense plan for Luzon just weeks earlier from top officials in Washington. MacArthur hoped that in the hills and thick jungles of Bataan, American and Filipino troops could hold out until the US sent more reinforcements and supplies.

Initially, direct responsibility for forces on Luzon fell to MacArthur's second-in-command, General Jonathan Wainwright. (Later, when Wainwright assumed overall command after MacArthur's evacuation, General Edward P. "Ned" King took charge in Bataan. Both King and Wainwright would become high-ranking POWs).

General MacArthur chose to set up his own headquarters on the fortified island of Corregidor at the strategic entrance to Manila Bay. As Japanese troops surged toward Manila, protected by their now-superior air power, it was time to put that plan into place.

Retreat. Delay. Hold on. And hope that help would arrive.

RETREAT! GET OUT!

EYEWITNESSES: AMEA WILLOUGHBY, LUCY WILSON, RALPH HIBBS, CARLOS ROMULO, CARL MYDANS

I t was the day before Christmas—a bright, sparkling day in Manila, out of key with the somber mood in our hearts and with the bad news that seemed to grow worse all the time," remembered American civilian Amea Willoughby.

Air raid sirens and bombings had become a fact of life, and Amea had come to dread them. By Christmas Eve, everyone knew Japanese forces would reach Manila soon; Filipino and American forces couldn't stop them. As we've seen, the attacks on Clark and Nichols airfields

A captured enemy war photo showing a Japanese air attack in progress.

and the Cavite Naval Base had stripped the Allies of air and sea power.

On December 24, Amea was at home making holiday care packages for hospital patients: soap, chocolate, and tobacco. Then her husband called. Woody told her General MacArthur had made a decision: It was time to get out of Manila before the Japanese arrived.

Woody Willoughby and his boss, Francis Sayre, the high commissioner, were America's highest-ranking officials in the Philippines, representing President Franklin D. Roosevelt. If they were captured, it would be useful Japanese propaganda and an insult directed right at the US president himself.

Amea and the others were instructed to go to the harbor, where a boat would take them and the Quezons, first family of the Philippines, to the fortified island of Corregidor. Located at the entrance to Manila Bay, the tadpole-shaped island nicknamed "the Rock" had long been used as a fortress for defense. Since the United States had taken control of the territory, the US government had made improvements, fortifying the island with roads, infrastructure, and a massive bomb-proof bunker complex called the Malinta Tunnel.

There was no better place to house General MacArthur's headquarters, along with President Quezon and his family, officers, and American diplomats. The Malinta Tunnel would become the last stand of the Americans on Luzon.

Amea and Woody rushed to the dock, and waited nervously to board a PT boat (patrol torpedo boat). "Trussed up in a gigantic life belt, I was told to jump in the water if the Japanese machine-gunned us," said Amea.

Amea felt numb with shock. A few weeks ago, she'd been looking forward to a festive holiday season. Now it was Christmas Eve and she might have to dive into the bay if she was shot at!

Everything had changed so quickly: the attacks, terrifying air raids that sent them scurrying to a basement bomb shelter, and now Japanese ground troops closing in on Manila. Amea realized their prospects for survival were dim. "It seemed unlikely to me that we would ever get off Corregidor except as prisoners—if we lived that long."

Army nurse Lucy Wilson was also on the move on Christmas Eve. The military nurses had been ordered to retreat, packing only what they could carry. A bus would take them to Limay, on the southeast side of the Bataan peninsula. There, they would get ready for the battle to come, as

A view of Malinta Hill on the island of Corregidor at the entrance to Manila Bay.

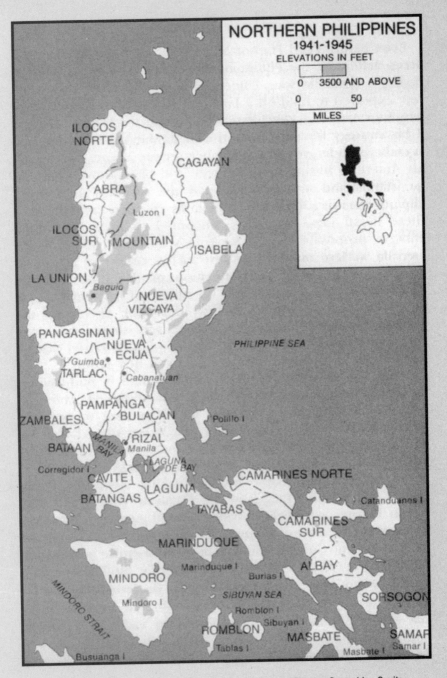

Here is the map of the Northern Philippines again; it shows Bataan, Corregidor, Cavite, and Manila. Note that north of Manila is the town of Cabanatuan. Nearby is the prison camp.

American and Filipino troops tried to hold off Japanese troops until the hoped-for reinforcements arrived.

On paper, Bataan made sense as the location for the Allied defensive position. The peninsula boasted thick jungle vegetation, rough terrain, and forests that would make attacks by air difficult. Some parts were mountainous. It was adjacent to Corregidor, at the entrance of Manila Bay, allowing for good access and communication between MacArthur's headquarters on the Rock and the troops.

On paper, troops could hold out—but only if a tremendous, coordinated effort in advance had brought in sufficient supplies of food and medicine to treat the debilitating tropical diseases so common in this region. For a variety of reasons, that effort had fallen far short. The dearth of adequate food and medicine would take a heavy toll.

And so, on Christmas Eve, Lucy boarded a bus for Hospital #1. (Lucy was later transferred to a second, makeshift facility called Hospital #2, also on Bataan.) She packed her white uniforms and hoped for the best. It was a long, slow journey. Each time enemy planes flew overhead, the nurses had to jump out of the bus and into muddy ditches to hide.

"We had nothing to eat all day, and arrived at Limay near midnight," Lucy remembered. "Someone opened some cans of beans and remarked it was Christmas Day!"

Lucy and the others had to adjust quickly to their new life. Right away, it was clear their white uniforms would be impossible to keep clean in the jungle. Instead, Lucy was issued a set of olive drab coveralls, obviously designed for male soldiers. "The seat came about to my knees and I weighed under 100 pounds."

In the desperate months ahead, as rations diminished and nurses and soldiers alike struggled with infections and diseases common in tropical jungle conditions, Lucy would end up weighing even less.

Christmas Eve found Dr. Ralph Hibbs headed into Manila for one last goodbye. He'd been on an advance assignment on Bataan, helping his battalion dig foxholes to prepare for the battle. A lot was at stake, food as well as medicine. The longer the American and Filipinos could hold onto Bataan, the more chance of help arriving from across the Pacific.

On Christmas Eve, when Ralph and a friend returned to Manila for supplies, he also hoped to meet up with his girlfriend, Pilar Campos. Once the fighting began, the young doctor knew he couldn't be sure when—or if—they'd ever see each other again. Ralph found Pilar at the newspaper where she worked, and they went to his apartment.

Pilar had already packed up Ralph's belongings into an army footlocker that had his name stenciled on it. She'd taken the locker home for safekeeping, not wanting it to fall into the possession of the enemy. At the time, neither Pilar nor Ralph realized the consequences this simple, friendly act would have.

As they parted, Ralph urged Pilar to leave the city and hide in the hills. He warned, "'Don't get mixed up in this mess.'"

Pilar Campos had no intention of running away.

Christmas Eve found Major Carlos Romulo in the headquarters of General Douglas MacArthur. Carlos was a
well-known journalist and newspaper publisher who began
reporting at age sixteen. Trusted both by President Manuel

As head of communications on General Douglas MacArthur's staff, Filipino journalist
Carlos Romulo served as spokesperson for the Voice of Freedom radio broadcasts, an
American radio program set up on Corregidor. It reached the Philippine public and sol-
diers on Bataan.

This photo was taken by American photographer Carl Mydans, who with his journalist
wife, Shelly, was captured by the Japanese and imprisoned for six months at Santo
Tomas University on the outskirts of Manila.

Quezon and General MacArthur, he'd been asked to serve MacArthur after the war started. His job was to keep the public informed, and in the days leading up to December 24, he rarely left his desk.

"I learned to work day and night, sustained by cat naps and by sandwiches and coffee wolfed at my desk," Carlos said. "I learned to raise my voice on the telephone so it could be heard over exploding bombs."

On December 24, MacArthur had met with President Quezon and they'd decided to declare Manila an open city, which was done on December 26. An open city meant the Allies wouldn't try to defend it. It was hoped that Manila being an open city would reduce bombing raids and avoid street fighting, the destruction of buildings, and most importantly, the deaths of innocent civilians.

In the midst of the chaos that day, Carlos had a clear memory of MacArthur promising that he would return to Manila. "'I'll be back, Carlos!'"

For the time being, though, MacArthur had left Carlos and a skeleton staff behind. With the enemy rapidly approaching, it was a frightening place to be.

"Christmas Eve—and we were left behind in an unprotected city, in a headquarters well known to the enemy planes still bombing our waterfront," Carlos said. "Phones rang constantly to report new tongues of Japanese troops licking their way down the hills and nearer Manila. Hundreds of enemy ships were vomiting more soldiers along our coasts. Platoons of Japanese tanks and flame throwers were rolling into the suburbs of Manila.

"At any moment we might be bombed. At any moment Japanese soldiers with drawn bayonets might charge through our undefended door. We didn't even have a jackknife among us."

MacArthur had promised to return. It was the same promise he'd make a few months later—after he was secreted to Australia when all hope of beating back Japan was lost. It remained to be seen whether the general could keep that promise.

A few days later, on New Year's Eve, Carlos received a phone call at home: He and other members of MacArthur's staff were being ordered to Corregidor to work out of headquarters there. Carlos kissed his wife, Virginia, and four sleeping sons goodbye.

As the family of a prominent Filipino, Carlos's wife and children were in grave danger and would have to go into hiding. For most of the next three years, Carlos had no news of them. His wife moved with the children to a small village, using her maiden name to avoid detection. (Fortunately, the family was reunited in the spring of 1945.)

202141

When Japan invaded the Philippines, thousands of civilians, including many American families with children, as seen on the facing page, were interned on the grounds of Santo Tomas University outside Manila. Some people built shanties and were able to grow vegetables, but food shortages and poor sanitation made for harsh living conditions.

NOT EVERYONE GOT OUT

Not everyone got out—and that included American photographer Carl Mydans and his wife, journalist Shelly Smith Mydans, who were both on assignment for *Life* magazine. While fellow journalists and newlyweds Mel and Annalee Jacoby were able to evacuate to Corregidor, the Mydans had no luck finding a boat.

"Early in the morning of January 2, the Japanese entered Manila. They came up boulevards in the predawn glow from the bay, riding on bicycles and on tiny motorcycles, their little flags with the one red ball looking like children's pennants. We had waited too long. It was too late, now, to get out," said Carl.

"It was late in the day when they took us. A truck came by loaded with other Americans and we were put aboard and driven to Santo Tomas University on the outskirts of Manila. We turned into the main gate of a great dusty compound, the sunset red behind us, and when we were ordered to dismount we jumped down with our suitcases and looked around us at the darkening grounds," he continued.

"Heaped about us were the gags and bundles of those who had come before us, their owners all moving aimlessly, seeming at cross purposes, flowing in and out of the gaunt building.

"The truck swung round and headed out of the compound and for a moment we stood where we were, looking after it, realizing we could not go that way ourselves.

"We were prisoners."

Carl and Shelly Mydans remained prisoners in the Philippines for eight months before being moved to Shanghai. From there, they were released in a prisoner exchange and returned to the United States in December 1943.

Carl did return to the Philippines, accompanying American soldiers when they liberated Santo Tomas in February 1945. We'll see what Carl found there later in the story.

STAYING ALIVE ON BATAAN

EYEWITNESSES: LUCY WILSON, RUBEN FLORES, RALPH HIBBS

For nurses like Lucy Wilson, the long months of fighting known as the Battle of Bataan became a desperate struggle to save lives—and stay alive herself—under harsh, unforgiving conditions.

In late January, Lucy had been transferred from Hospital #1 to Hospital #2 on the peninsula. Hospital #1 had been planned in advance, but the second field hospital was a makeshift affair. A narrow dirt road had been cut through dense tropical vegetation to bring in supplies and people. Latrines for the nurses were dug the very evening the women arrived. A local carpenter constructed furniture—tables, medicine cabinets, and beds—all from bamboo.

The nurses had little privacy. They slept in cots under mosquito nets and bathed in a nearby stream. Lucy served in the operating room: a tent. "Sometimes when bombs and shells landed we wondered if the tent wasn't going to fall down, it shook so bad," she said.

Lucy hadn't been trained in battlefield nursing, but she quickly adapted. The fierce fighting meant doctors and nurses worked long hours without breaks. Lucy always knew when the next wounded would arrive. "We would see the firing in the distance and figure about how many hours—usually one to four—before we would be receiving more patients."

Meals under these conditions were irregular. Besides, there wasn't much to eat as the weeks went by and supplies continued to dwindle. "We only ate twice a day and that consisted mostly of rice with weevils in it stored since 1918, and anything else that could be scrounged up," Lucy said.

It's no wonder she got sick. Yet Lucy managed to handle even this situation with good humor. "Eating everything we could get our hands on, we all had diarrhea. One day, I ran behind a bush and hurriedly took down my coveralls and started to vomit at the same time I was having diarrhea," she recalled. "I heard a noise and looked around to see a huge iguana lizard looking at me."

Intestinal diseases and malaria affected almost everyone. "The average diet now was about 1500 calories and I'm sure soldiers at the front lines didn't always get that much," Lucy said. "The physical exertion in the heat and rough monotonous terrain with creeping thorny vines left a person wet with perspiration and extreme thirst."

. . .

Rations were soon reduced even more, something Ruben Flores, a cook with the 200th Coast Artillery, remembered well.

In an oral history interview years later, Ruben recalled the frustration of having to make do with less and less. "At first the food was all right, but we couldn't get more than half rations."

Even those rations were cut. Ruben explained, "The quartermaster [officer in charge of supplies] would send in some food for us once a week. I remember we were getting carabao [water buffalo] meat . . . and then they quit sending carabao . . . and started issuing horsemeat." This horsemeat came initially from slaughtered Filipino cavalry horses, but again, it wasn't enough.

Ruben had grown up in Las Cruces, New Mexico, and served in the merchant marines before the war. He was stationed in New York when it came time to enlist. But his heart was in New Mexico. Ruben wanted to serve with friends and fellow Latinos, so he became part of New Mexico's 200th Coast Artillery with others from his home state. The 200th Coast Artillery also included later additions such as Hank Cowan, who was reassigned to the unit after the bombers he had worked on at Clark Field were destroyed.

The 200th Coast Artillery was charged with attacking Japanese planes during their bombing raids on Bataan, but a lack of good ammunition and equipment hampered that effort. "Mentally, it was devastating . . . We were supposed to defend against air attacks, but we had old-type ammo with

17-second fuses," Ruben said. "The Japanese figured that out. We couldn't reach them."

Along with rapidly depleting food supplies and poor ammunition, the shortage of medicine, especially quinine used to treat malaria, was a major issue on Bataan. Malaria is a disease caused by a protozoan parasite that invades the red blood cells and causes fevers and chills; some severe forms can be fatal. The parasites are transmitted to humans by female *Anopheles* mosquitoes.

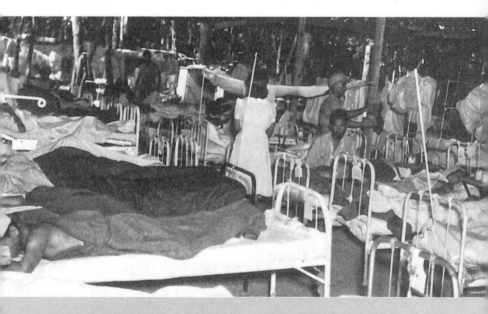

A field hospital under the trees on the Bataan peninsula in 1942. Many soldiers suffered from gas gangrene, a tissue-killing, life-threatening condition caused by bacteria infecting their wounds. While this Filipina nurse is wearing white, the nurses in Lucy Wilson's group switched to coveralls.

(Malaria is still a threat to many people in the world. Newer therapies now exist, but during World War II, quinine, which kills the parasites, was the main treatment available.)

Lucy Wilson saw sick soldiers everywhere she looked. "By the end of March, I think, 75 to 80% of the front line had malaria. Dengue fever, scurvy, beriberi, amoebic dysentery, common diarrhea and dysentery, hookworms, and other intestinal parasites, in addition to injuries, were taking their toll."

Since his first battle on Bataan in early January, Dr. Ralph Hibbs had seen firsthand the impact of injuries, disease, and malnutrition on soldiers in combat. As a battalion surgeon,

Soldiers in an anti-tank company on the Bataan peninsula try to hold their positions during the Battle of Bataan in early 1942.

Ralph's place was in the midst of battle, providing immediate care before wounded soldiers could be brought (or walk on their own) to a hospital in the rear.

"We never had IV fluids in front line combat situations. About a dozen of my men were in the [aid] station—tagging, applying tourniquets, compressing wounds to stop bleeding, giving hypos and oral medications, washing and bandaging, fitting slings, assisting litter teams from the front and those sneaking to the rear," Ralph explained.

In one ferocious battle in mid-January 1942, Ralph and his team struggled to keep up with the casualties. "The fighting was intense with mortars, artillery, diver bombers and automatic weapons fire," he said.

The thick jungle terrain made the situation chaotic and confusing. "Night came and about the same time, silence. A hot sultry haze came over the cane field . . . The ravine was full of wounded with a few drifting to the rear," said Ralph.

A captured war photo shows a Japanese tank camouflaged by trees in 1942.

"Moans were heard from the unconscious men, otherwise, everything was quiet."

During his first experience of combat in early January, Ralph had "done nothing except to panic in my foxhole, cowering like a rat burdened with the helplessness of our situation."

Just a few weeks later, the twenty-six-year-old doctor had become calm and competent, coordinating litter teams and evacuations by ambulance. "We made judgment calls on the patient's prognosis, which determined priorities for evacuation. Our main effort was directed to those we felt would recover."

And so it went—through January, February, and all of March. Casualties increased. The food ration decreased. "In January it [the daily ration] averaged roughly 2,000 calories, then dropped to 1,500 by February and 1,000 during March," said Ralph. By the end, the ration was less than 1,000 calories, consisting of "two double handfuls of rice, a small portion of canned fruit, a couple ounces of canned fish, an occasional hunk of meat, and rarely, a few ounces of evaporated milk."

On April 8, 1942, after weeks on the front lines of battles, the surrender order was announced, marking a bitter end to a long, hard-fought campaign.

Ralph and several members of his medical team trudged to a location near Hospital #1. Now they'd have to choose whether to remain on duty and report to Colonel James Duckworth, the chief medical officer in charge of Hospital #1—or take their chances and escape into the jungle to avoid capture.

An April 1942 photo shows the destruction caused by Japanese bombs and shells on Bataan.

"I felt weak and choleric from too much walking and not enough food. Weary, foot sore, hungry and bewildered, the six of us had been without hot food for three days. My guts ached, yet the realization of the end to this damn jungle massacre evoked a relief," said Ralph.

And then, unexpectedly, the decision was taken out of his hands. "Suddenly I began to chill, my teeth rattled, my bones ached, I had malaria! Taking two aspirin, cuddling up in a ball, I realized the door to escape had just slammed shut."

Ralph knew he wouldn't survive long in the jungle without quinine and so he made the decision to surrender. "Later that very night I woke up with the earth shaking and the trees swishing. 'You'd think it was an earthquake,' I muttered raising up on one elbow."

It was.

Lucy Wilson also felt the earthquake the night of April 8. She'd been looking forward to the next day for a special reason: She was supposed to get married!

Before arriving in the Philippines, Lucy had been on active duty in El Paso, Texas, where she'd dated a soldier named Dan Jopling. Dan had been sent to the Philippines with his unit in the fall of 1941. The two had managed to meet several times and had fallen in love.

Even on Bataan, Dan had been able to visit a few times, and in March he'd asked Lucy to marry him. He didn't have a ring, but gave her a bracelet. "I wore it till I got so skinny it would slip down my arm and I was afraid I might contaminate the surgical field, so I took it off," Lucy said.

The couple decided to marry the next time Dan could arrange to visit her: April 9. Lucy and Dan would always remember the date, but for a different reason entirely.

"By April, hunger and disease were greater enemies than the Japanese," Lucy remembered. "In the last days, many left sick-beds to fight. Many were too weak to carry machine guns through the jungle and steep ravines . . . everyone fought to the last ditch."

In April, rumors began to spread about a possible surrender, a capitulation no soldier on Bataan wanted, but was powerless to avoid. Late on the evening of April 8, Lucy got word that General Jonathan Wainwright, who now commanded the

Bataan forces, was ordering the nurses to Corregidor. It could mean only one thing: Surrender was imminent.

Lucy had no choice but to obey, but abandoning her patients that night was one of the hardest things she'd ever done. "Walking out in the middle of an operation with hundreds lined up under the trees waiting for surgery was devastating to me," she said. "This I have to live with for the rest of my life."

Lucy left so quickly she wasn't able to bring Dan's bracelet with her. She and several other nurses were among the last to reach the shore. There they discovered that they'd already missed the boat to Corregidor scheduled for midnight. The young women waited on the beach all night, not knowing

Houses of Filipino civilians burning during the assault on Bataan.

whether they'd be rescued by friends or captured by enemy soldiers.

"An earthquake shook the ground, to add a little more discomfort," said Lucy. Around noon on April 9, they got lucky. "A boat came by and saw us sitting there and picked us up and took us to Corregidor."

It was April 9, 1942: the fall of Bataan. "This was the day Dan was supposed to have come for us to get married," said Lucy. "The rest of the day I watched the shelling and bombing of Bataan, wondering if he could possibly survive that inferno."

Soldiers all over Bataan got the news. Ruben Flores never forgot what his lieutenant told them: "'We are not surrendering, *we have been surrendered.*'"

GENERAL WAINWRIGHT'S HORSE

General Jonathan M. "Skinny" Wainwright (1883–1953) was a career army officer, already fifty-eight when World War II broke out. Born into a military family, Wainwright had a deep love of horses and had served as a cavalry instructor. He was the senior commanding officer under General Douglas MacArthur in the Philippines and took charge after MacArthur left. Captured on Corregidor in May 1942, Wainwright became the highest-ranking American POW of World War II. He later received the Medal of Honor.

Among the horses in the Twenty-Sixth Cavalry on Bataan was Wainwright's own beloved jumper, Little Boy. As conditions worsened, fodder for the animals began to run low. At the same time, the need for more food for the troops had become desperate.

When an officer approached him about the shortage, Wainwright didn't hesitate. He gave the order with tears in his eyes. "'Captain, you will begin killing the horses at once. Little Boy is the horse you will kill first.'"

CORREGIDOR: IN THE TUNNEL

EYEWITNESSES: LUCY WILSON, AMEA WILLOUGHBY, CARLOS ROMULO

O n April 9, 1942, the day Allied forces surrendered on Bataan, Lucy Wilson got her first look at the Malinta Tunnel on Corregidor, "the Rock."

Corregidor Island, just three and a half miles long, and a little over a mile across at its widest point, had for centuries been a defense fortress for the Philippines, perfectly positioned to guard Manila Bay. By 1942, it was fortified with guns pointing west toward the South China Sea. The Rock was just a short distance from the shore of the Bataan peninsula, making it ideal for General Douglas MacArthur's headquarters—and the final stronghold against complete Japanese control of Luzon.

The tunnel might have seemed daunting to folks like Amea Willoughby and Carlos Romulo, who'd arrived on Corregidor straight from clean, comfortable homes, but to Lucy even the smelly, stuffy, dirty Malinta Tunnel was an improvement after several months in the jungle.

"Life in the Malinta Tunnel was not so bad for me as Bataan; we had solid rock over our heads," she said.

That didn't mean conditions were great. Since there weren't enough beds, two nurses shared a single cot, sleeping in shifts. Lucy worked in the hospital at night. When she got off duty, the other nurse who was her bunkmate was already up.

Douglas MacArthur (left) and his chief of staff, Richard Sutherland, confer in the Malinta Tunnel ten days before MacArthur was evacuated to Australia on March 11, 1942. Journalist Carlos Romulo remembered the strong bond of trust between the two men. Once, Carlos woke in the tunnel to hear Sutherland on the phone, presumably to an officer on Bataan, "shouting in a voice that might have been MacArthur's own: 'I tell you to hold that line! If you don't I'll go over there and hold it myself!'"

"Heat and the odor of the hospital and bodies, and flies and insects added to the discomfort," she said. "Hospital beds were triple decked. Laundry was limited for lack of water and there was no place to hang sheets or clothing."

A wondrous feat of engineering, the Malinta Tunnel, built by the US Army Corps of Engineers in the 1930s, consisted of a main tunnel more than eight hundred feet long, about twenty-four feet wide, and eighteen feet high. Within Malinta a labyrinth of connecting tunnels contained a hospital, military headquarters, cots for sleeping, and space for storage.

To Amea Willoughby the complex seemed like "a giant anthill. When the [bombing] raids came nobody inside needed the warning red signal lights to inform them, for the crowds surged in from outdoors and the general atmosphere of busy briskness was replaced by a wary, tense inaction."

The tunnel was damp, smoky, smelly, and noisy. Although there was electricity from a small power plant on Corregidor, it wasn't reliable and the tunnel was sometimes in total darkness. Water was in short supply.

"There wasn't enough room, enough bedding, enough of anything in the tunnel, except smells, bedbugs, and flies," remembered journalist Carlos Romulo. "Not even all the officers had cots. The soldiers slept where the night found them, and those who could not find room in the caves slept out under the trees where they were exposed to bombs . . . Suffocate or be bombed—you had your choice."

These views of the Malinta Tunnel on Corregidor show its size. The photos date from March 1945 when General Douglas MacArthur (left in the close-up entering the tunnel) returned, three years after being evacuated from Corregidor in March 1942.

Carlos had arrived on New Year's Day with three uniforms. After visiting soldiers in the foxholes of Bataan and seeing their ragged clothing, "on my next visit I carried two of my uniforms to give away. Soon I, too, was in rags . . .

"In the tunnel one of our poorer jokes was repeated over and over, when at night we stood the remains of our socks on their toeless ends, held our nose, and shouted, 'Look, guys, they can walk by themselves,'" he recalled.

"The tunnel was dirty, our beds were dirty, and we were dirty . . . Sometimes when I could not sleep I would turn my flashlight on under the covers and watch an echelon of thirty or forty bedbugs marching across my steadily shrinking stomach."

As the bombing raids on Corregidor intensified, so did the number of wounded, and Amea admired the nurses who labored under these harsh conditions. "A nurse's work is undoubtedly one of the toughest of all war jobs, calling for an almost superhuman physical and mental stamina. Corregidor nurses were magnificent," she wrote. "They were a vital part of the war."

Carlos Romulo remembered one raid blasting a machine shop on Corregidor. The attack killed thirteen men and wounded thirty-five others. "The ambulances raced between bombs over the Rock to rescue the dead and wounded. All that afternoon the bombs kept falling and the ambulances came and went in the tunnel, disgorging their terrible cargoes, hurrying off for another load . . .

"We transferred the Voice of Freedom [radio station] to a booth in the tunnel, beside the hospital entrance. The procession into the hospital became part of the daily scene. But I never got used to seeing the men carried past."

Most books about Bataan and Corregidor focus on male military leaders and soldiers. But nurses like Lucy Wilson and diplomatic spouse Amea Willoughby, who'd been evacuated to Corregidor on December 24, remind us that women (and kids) were there too.

Staying in an arm of the tunnel along with Amea was Aurora Quezon, wife of the president of the Philippines, along with her two young adult daughters. Carlos Romulo remembered how the eldest, Maria Aurora, nicknamed "Baby," volunteered every day in the tunnel hospital, making up beds. Jean MacArthur, Douglas MacArthur's wife, was on the island with her young son, Arthur. High Commissioner Francis Sayre and his wife had a fifteen-year-old son named Billy.

Corregidor was under siege from the moment Amea arrived. She hadn't liked bombing raids in Manila. This was worse. Although the tunnel was safe, soldiers assigned to AA (antiaircraft) guns elsewhere on the island were at risk. Even stepping outside the tunnel to eat or go for a walk and get a breath of fresh air could be dangerous.

"The first time I was under shellfire I was more lucky than wise," said Amea. "It was still so early in the morning that the faint freshness that marked the change from cool night to the steamy day still lingered in the air. Sitting on a pile of planks a few hundred feet up from the tunnel, I was enjoying a moment of solitude.

"Round the bend, walking slowly toward me, came four tired soldiers. Laden with gear, helmets on the backs of their heads, they trudged along, raising little puffs of dust with each footstep.

"Suddenly the still morning was pierced by a shrill, screaming whistle. On the road directly in front of me the soldiers collapsed like a pack of cards and flattened themselves to the earth. Paralyzed, I continued to sit there . . ."

Afterward, one freckled-face young soldier turned to her. "'Say, lady,' he said calmly, 'can't you lay down faster?'"

Before long, Amea could flatten herself with the best of them. "Once I even beat a Marine to the ground, but he claimed it was because I didn't have as far to go."

Lucy Wilson never met Amea Willoughby or Carlos Romulo. By the time Lucy arrived on April 9, both had gotten out. Amea was evacuated by submarine in February 1942. And on the evening of April 8, as Lucy was making her way toward the shore to wait for a boat to Corregidor, Carlos was embarking on a treacherous journey in the opposite direction, as we'll soon see.

Another person had left Corregidor by the time Lucy Wilson arrived: General Douglas MacArthur himself.

All winter, Carlos and everyone else had been hoping that reinforcements would arrive for the troops on Bataan. "Our main talk was about these reinforcements," said Carlos. "It never occurred to us to doubt that help was on the way."

And still no reinforcements came. Then, on March 11, 1942, General Richard Sutherland, MacArthur's chief of staff, asked Carlos to meet with him. They stood outside in the corner of a tent, with soldiers carrying garbage hurrying out past them from the tunnel hospital.

"What Sutherland had to tell me was the worst news I had heard since Pearl Harbor," Carlos recalled. "First he explained it was to be kept strictly confidential.

"Then he said, 'General MacArthur has been ordered out by the first available transportation. He is leaving Corregidor tonight.'"

Carlos went back into the tunnel and sat slumped at his desk. He wondered how he could explain this when he next went to offer encouragement to soldiers in the foxholes of Bataan.

At that moment, he felt a hand on his shoulder. MacArthur had come to offer Carlos a choice: Go to Australia or remain. A part of Carlos longed to be safely off Corregidor. Because of his Voice of Freedom radio broadcasts, the Japanese had put a price on his head. If Carlos was captured, he would be executed. His family was already in hiding.

"But the carrying of reports to the boys on the front lines and the radio work had to be carried on," said Carlos. "We were talking as big as ever over the Voice of Freedom, making liars of the Japanese propagandists and trying to assuage the fears of those who dared to listen."

His countrymen depended on these radio broadcasts to give them hope. He had to keep going as long as he possibly could. Carlos made his decision.

"I said, 'I'll stay.'

"MacArthur smiled. 'I knew you'd say that, Carlos. The Voice of Freedom can't be stilled. It must go on. It's our voice.'"

MacArthur had sworn not to desert his men. He'd resisted earlier requests from officials in Washington to leave. This time, though, he'd had no choice. Roosevelt had given him a direct order, and the president was, of course, commander-in-chief.

Later, one presidential advisor observed that Roosevelt understood full well that MacArthur's departure would leave thousands of American and Filipino soldiers feeling abandoned. "'It was ordering the captain to be the first to leave the sinking ship.'"

But the ship *was* sinking. And so on the night of March 11, MacArthur departed secretly by PT boat to Mindanao Island and then by submarine across the Pacific, taking aides and top military staff with him. MacArthur would command operations in the southwest Pacific from his headquarters in Australia. President Quezon, ailing from the tuberculosis that would end his life in 1944, had already been secreted to safety with his family.

Among MacArthur's staff members left behind were Carlos Romulo and General Jonathan Wainwright, who assumed overall command and moved from Bataan to the Corregidor headquarters; General Edward "Ned" King was put in direct charge of Bataan.

The harsh fate about to befall the Philippines became even more apparent once MacArthur arrived in Australia and learned of the discussions that had been taking place at the highest levels. The Arcadia Conference, held in Washington, DC, December 22, 1941, to January 14, 1942, had brought Allied leaders together. Roosevelt hadn't been able to ignore the appeals of Prime Minister Winston Churchill to come to Great Britain's aid to defeat Adolf Hitler.

The war in Europe was simply a higher priority. And even there, it would take time, many battles, and a massive war production effort and mobilization of troops until the Allies were able to return to France and mount a final effort to defeat the Nazis and liberate Europe. (The Allied invasion of Normandy was, of course, D-Day, June 6, 1944.)

No, MacArthur hadn't had a choice. At the same, the general realized that his departure—and America's abandonment—was a devastating blow to the US troops left behind, and the loyal Filipino soldiers fighting beside them.

In Australia, when asked for a statement by reporters, MacArthur spoke of his remarkable escape across the Pacific. Then he vowed to devote himself wholeheartedly to organizing the American offensive against Japan, with the goal of complete victory in the Pacific and the recapture of the Philippines.

MacArthur closed with his famous promise: *"'I came through and I shall return.'"*

It would be a long way back.

Amea and Woody Willoughby also evacuated Corregidor, escaping in late February. While we've gotten to know Amea here, Woody also played a fascinating role in the story of the Philippines in the war: Woody was in charge of saving the territory's gold.

The work began before the Japanese invasion, when Woody's team made a huge effort to record and keep track of gold and securities (stock certificates) from the national treasury and move everything from Manila to a vault on Corregidor.

On February 4, 1942, the USS *Trout* slipped through the Japanese blockade to the dock on Corregidor. The bars of gold had to be loaded onto the submarine before dawn. The skipper was happy to oblige: Since the submarine was bringing in cases and cases of AA (antiaircraft) ammunition, the heavy gold would serve as ballast on the return trip.

Woody and others on Corregidor were ready. "The bars were brought from the vault in cars and everyone took a hand with the loading. Hour on hour they worked in the darkness, heavy, steady labor, with not a second to lose," said Amea.

"Over the dock and across a teetering gangplank the gold was carried. Some of it was thrown from hand to hand, chain-fashion. Hurry, hurry, but don't drop any. Keep your balance, fellow. They packed it in the torpedo rooms and under the bunks, wherever there was room."

That night, the men ran out of time before they could load boxes containing securities. They concocted a plan to meet the submarine the next night to finish. Dawn brought a tense waiting time, as Amea and Woody scanned the skies, hoping the submarine lingering nearby wouldn't be spotted.

When darkness fell, Woody and two others set off on a boat with the valuable records. Yet when they reached the appointed rendezvous, no submarine could be found. Time passed.

"For three hours they searched and waited, churning the screw of the little launch so that the listening device of the submarine could pick up the sound. They searched the night for the solid outlines of the submarine with waning hope," said Amea.

"Finally, when they were about to give up, the dark hulk materialized off the port bow and the launch came alongside. By that time the water was so rough that the two crafts see-sawed dangerously up and down. Somehow the securities were got on board."

The next day, as he examined the now-empty vault, Woody found something left behind: a tiny bar of gold no bigger than a matchbox.

"He remembered how hard everyone had worked and how they had tried to avoid the slightest mistake. He sighed and put the tiny bar of gold into his briefcase," Amea recalled.

In late February, Amea and Woody and eight other civilians, including High Commissioner Francis Sayre and his family, escaped Corregidor by submarine. Amea had never imagined traveling in a submarine across the Pacific in the midst of war. But she was ready. "Our instructions were to wear slacks and 'be prepared for anything.'"

Amea adapted well to life under the sea as the submarine crawled through enemy waters. Once, she got a chance to peek at the Dutch East Indies (now Indonesia) through the periscope. After a tense journey, they reached Australia safely, where Amea treated herself to a bath, followed by a shopping trip to purchase real fruit and vegetables. Amea found herself mesmerized by a window display of succulent pears, golden peaches, and snowy cauliflowers.

"I stood there before the window for some time before I realized that actually I had the power to buy some of what

I looked at with such longing," she remembered. "Knowing that I could really buy a whole bunch of grapes made me feel tremendously rich."

Amea and Woody made the final leg of their long journey home by ship, escorted by a navy destroyer. "As soon as we landed, Woody hurried to the Federal Reserve Bank in San Francisco to confer with the officials about the gold and securities that had been sent from Corregidor," she recalled.

All the records had been checked meticulously. At first, Woody was celebrated, but soon it became clear something was amiss. Amea recalled that after hemming and hawing for a while, the officials at last revealed the problem. "Mind you, they said, it was a marvelous accomplishment to have saved so many millions, *but*, they were short one small piece of gold the size of a matchbox, and worth about $306.

"Throughout this long approach to the main topic Woody had listened with interest. Now he unfastened the straps of his briefcase and took out the little gold bar. 'Oh, that!' he said, and gave it them."

That night, Woody and Amea and other escapees had the chance to speak on a shortwave radio broadcast back to Bataan and Corregidor. They weren't sure if they'd be heard.

"The memory of Corregidor was vivid in all our minds. We could see again the hospital outlet where three or four of the men would undoubtedly be bent over the dials, trying to establish good reception from the United States. At the gun batteries the vigilant crews would perhaps be trying to hear.

But how could we know? If an attack was in progress nobody would be able to listen or to think about anything beyond the job of the moment."

Each person said something a little different, but Amea thought everyone tried to convey the message they knew all those left behind longed to hear.

"'You are not forgotten here,' we told them."

SEE THE GOLD!

To view pictures of gold being unloaded off the USS *Trout* (SS-202), visit http://www.navsource.org/archives/08/08202. htm. The USS *Trout* and her crew were lost on patrol two years later.

INCIDENTS OF LIFE
IN THE TUNNEL

Amea Willoughby wasn't a journalist, but her book, *I Was on Corregidor*, is a valuable primary source about life in the Malinta Tunnel during the siege of 1942. She tells human stories that otherwise would be lost but now allow us, decades later, to better understand what that time was like for some of those who lived through it.

It's a reminder to pick up your pencil, tap on your keyboard, make a video—and tell stories about *your* life.

NINI QUEZON'S CANARY

Amea Willoughby discovered that the animals on Corregidor were as frightened by the shelling attacks as she was. Once, a wild monkey raced into the tunnel during a bomb attack and stayed quite close to her. Another time, she shared a ditch with a cat.

But pets weren't allowed in Malinta Tunnel, so when Amea heard a canary singing one morning a few days after she arrived, she wondered if the stress had gotten to her.

"Of course there couldn't be a canary on Corregidor, I thought, and certainly not in the tunnel," said Amea. "Still, penetrating, sweet trills and whistles rang in the air. I thought maybe the walls had some queer acoustic effects, so I lay down again. Again a burst of song. It certainly did sound like a canary.

"The last few days had been a strain, so I said to myself severely, 'Pull yourself together. This is no time to be hearing canaries . . .'

"It was not till two days later, when the floors were being mopped, that out from under Nini Quezon's bed came a bird-cage with a canary in it."

The daughter of the Philippine president was twenty at the time. Nini went on to live a remarkable life as an activist and defender of human rights. Her father died of tuberculosis in 1944. Tragically, in 1949, her mother; sister Maria Aurora, "Baby," a law student; and Nini's first husband were assassinated in an attack. Nini was spared only because she was pregnant and had stayed home because she hadn't been feeling well. Nini married again and passed away in July 2021 at age one hundred, leaving behind nine children and many grandchildren.

ANNALEE JACOBY, WAR CORRESPONDENT

Annalee Jacoby, a war correspondent for *Time* and *Life* magazines, was also living in the Malinta Tunnel in early 1942 along with her new husband, Mel. The couple evacuated from Corregidor to Australia in February; Mel was killed there in April 1942 in an accident on an airfield tarmac.

Amea Willoughby mentions Annalee in her account, and clearly admired the young, self-reliant journalist pursuing her passion as a war correspondent. Amea recalled that newlywed Annalee had arrived without a traditional bridal trousseau, and instead acquired a pair of oversize men's khaki pants. "We were impressed, and some of us were envious, of her arm band which said PRESS."

Want to know more about Annalee? The Jacobys' story is told in a book called *Eve of a Hundred Midnights: The Star-Crossed Love Story of Two WWII Correspondents and Their Epic Escape Across the Pacific,* by Bill Lascher.

SURRENDER: FIRST BATAAN, THEN CORREGIDOR

EYEWITNESSES: HANK COWAN, CARLOS ROMULO, LUCY WILSON, RALPH HIBBS

The fall of the Philippines didn't happen all at once. The main Allied forces on Bataan fell on April 9, 1942; Corregidor toppled on May 6. It would be June 9 before the last scattered Allied forces on other islands officially surrendered. The truth was, though, the defeat at the Battle of Bataan spelled the end of hope for the Allies in the Philippines.

Some Filipino and American soldiers on Bataan escaped to take their chances as guerrilla soldiers behind enemy lines. Most did not. From a prewar army strength of about 120,000, more than 70,000 (approximately 58,000 Filipino troops and nearly 12,000 American soldiers on Bataan) became prisoners of war, and their even more terrible ordeal began.

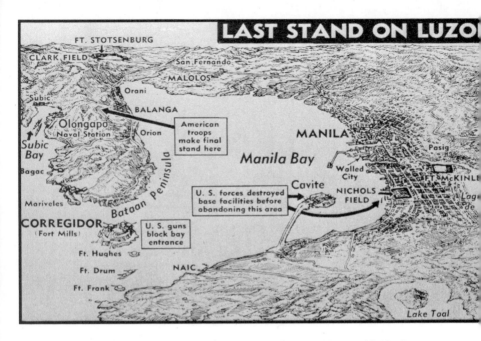

This map shows key sites on Luzon, including Clark and Nichols airfields, the navy base at Cavite, the Bataan Peninsula, and Corregidor. After the April 9, 1942, surrender on Bataan, American and Filipino soldiers were forced to march from Mariveles to San Fernando in what became known as the Bataan Death March. Corregidor held on until May 6.

The Battle of Bataan had been a discouraging struggle for Private Hank Cowan. After the attack on Clark Field, Hank had been assigned to the 200th Coast Artillery, the outfit made up of New Mexico National Guard members. The retreat to Bataan hadn't come as a surprise to Hank, and he was never optimistic about their chances.

"There was no doubt in my mind that Bataan was to be our last battle," he said. "With the Japanese virtually in control of the South Pacific I could see no way we could receive help. The only thing we could do was to fight as long as possible."

Fight as long as possible—to the very last ditch. And that's what American and Filipino forces did, despite being beset by hunger and disease.

"By March 1942, about 80% of our front line troops were sick with malaria and our food supplies and medicine were running out fast," Hank recalled. "My squadron was issued six cans of salmon for 100 men. The ammunition was also running low.

"We prayed that somehow the good old USA would send some help. We still could not realize that our country could not help us. Each night the sound of battle came closer and closer. We heard that General MacArthur had been ordered to Australia and General Wainwright would take over. I knew that something important would happen soon."

Early in the evening of April 8, Hank and his unit were ordered to move to the town of Mariveles on the tip of the Bataan Peninsula. "We walked all night and as we walked we knew that something dreadful had happened. Everything in the world seemed to be blowing up around us," said Hank.

Like Lucy Wilson and Ralph Hibbs, Hank felt the earthquake that night. "It seemed like the end of the world. A few hours later the ground shook again, like another earthquake, but we learned later that our commanders had been ordered to destroy all remaining ammunition and supplies to keep them from falling into enemy hands. We walked as far as we could go and there was nowhere else to go. This was the end.

General Masaharu Homma was in charge of the assault of the Philippines. Victory in the Philippines took longer than anticipated, and was more costly in casualties, equipment, and men. The prolonged fight in Bataan delayed Japan's military timetable, which displeased Homma's superiors and resulted in his being recalled to Japan and sidelined.

"Soon the word was passed for us to surrender and await further orders. This was the saddest day of my life. I cried in frustration," said Hank. "General Masaharu Homma had launched an all out attack on the front line with a terrific artillery and air attack, followed by a tank and infantry assault.

"The American and Filipino troops could not hold out any longer."

Despite the courageous tenacity of soldiers, nurses, and doctors, the disastrous outcome on Bataan had never really been in doubt. Historian Louis Morton observed that "the Pacific Fleet, which was to have fought its way through to them by that time, never arrived. The fate of the Philippine garrison had been decided on the opening day of the war, at Pearl Harbor."

Morton went on: "The battle for Bataan was ended; the fighting was over. The men who had survived the long ordeal could feel justly proud of their accomplishment. For three months they had held off the Japanese, only to be overwhelmed finally by disease and starvation . . . Each man had done his best and none need feel shame.

"The events that followed General [Ned] King's surrender present a confused and chaotic story of the disintegration and dissolution of a starved, diseased, and beaten army," he wrote.

The soldiers would always be known by the nickname "the battling bastards of Bataan," a term coined from a limerick written by an American journalist named Frank Hewlett who was working in Manila. The poem came to symbolize the abandonment they felt.

We're the Battling Bastards of Bataan,
No Mama, No Papa, No Uncle Sam
No aunts, no uncles, no cousins, no nieces,
No pills, no planes, no artillery pieces,
And nobody gives a damn!

This captured Japanese war photo shows dejected American military leaders, with General Ned King in the center, as they discuss the surrender of Filipino and American troops on Bataan in April 1942 with Japanese military leaders. General King tried to convey the poor physical condition of the men, but was not able to convince his Japanese counterpart to use American trucks to transport prisoners to camps in the north.

Now these valiant soldiers faced something even more horrific. Morton wrote that they "had earned the right to be treated with consideration and decency, but their enemies had reserved for them even greater privations and deeper humiliation than any they had yet suffered on Bataan."

When we pick up Hank Cowan's story in Part Two, we'll see just how true that was. After all he had endured so far, the worst was still to come.

You may remember that the night before the surrender of Bataan, Lucy Wilson had been ordered away from the operating table to try to catch a boat for her retreat from the Malinta Tunnel on Corregidor. On that same evening, Chief Press Relations

Officer Carlos Romulo was headed from Corregidor back *into* Bataan, in a nail-biting, last-minute attempt to escape.

Carlos had remained at his post, even when General Douglas MacArthur had given him the chance to escape to Australia in March. He'd stayed, enduring bombing, diminishing food supplies, and bouts of diarrhea and fever. He risked boat trips to Bataan to speak with young Filipino soldiers just seventeen or eighteen; soldiers who reminded him of his own boys.

So long as it was possible, Carlos wrote and delivered Voice of Freedom radio broadcasts from a small booth near the entrance to the Malinta Tunnel. Once, just as he was about to enter, a huge bomb hit the hill outside.

"Everyone in the place was knocked flat," said Carlos. "I got up and went into the booth. Dust was rolling in from sandbags split open before the entrance, and over everything hung the bitter scent of picric acid [a military explosive]. Everyone was coughing, their throats made raw by the penetrating fumes."

Carlos looked at his watch. He had seventeen minutes until the noon broadcast. He finished writing the script.

At four o'clock on the afternoon of April 8, 1942, Carlos was summoned to General Jonathan Wainwright's headquarters in a lateral shoot of the Malinta Tunnel. Carlos saluted and Wainwright stood. Carlos later wrote that the general looked tired and worn.

"'Colonel Romulo, I'm ordering you out of Corregidor.'

"I was bewildered. I knew no planes or boats were leaving now for the mainland. I asked, 'What do you mean?'"

General Wainwright told him, "'Bataan is hopeless.'"

Then he handed Carlos an envelope with secret orders. Carlos was to depart Corregidor at seven o'clock that night on a small launch to Bataan and make his way to the Bataan airfield. A small plane would be waiting there to bring him to Mindanao Island, where he was to report to American generals. The orders had been radioed to Wainwright from General MacArthur in Australia.

It was, perhaps, a foolhardy attempt. But neither MacArthur nor President Manuel Quezon wanted to risk the capture of the fiercely loyal, talented Carlos, who had begun as a journalist at age sixteen and in 1942 would win a Pulitzer Prize for reporting. (They were right: After the war, Carlos enjoyed a long and distinguished career, serving eight presidents of the Philippines and representing his country at the United Nations.)

"I was the last man out of Bataan," Carlos wrote later. "I escaped from that bloody trap because the Japanese had set a price upon my head and because General Douglas MacArthur was able to arrange my last-minute rescue in a makeshift amphibian [aircraft] nicknamed "the Duck." The obsolete crate could not rise seventy feet above Manila Bay, while Japanese ack-ack shells and machine-gun bullets brightened the night around us—the night of April 8–9, 1942, that saw the fall of Bataan."

Although the orders were secret, Carlos's friends in the tunnel soon figured out that something was afoot. Several people pressed hastily written letters on him for loved ones. Everyone knew that once Bataan fell, Corregidor would be next.

Carlos felt full of guilt as he looked at doctors and nurses still battling to save lives, and at the young soldiers trying to grab a few minutes of rest in the tunnel. When he had tried to protest that he couldn't go, General Wainwright had snapped, "'You're under orders.'"

And so Carlos left. "The little launch was waiting with drumming motors beside the dock," he remembered. "I sat in the boat looking back at my friends on the Rock, and I hope I never know a moment as heavy as that again . . ."

The short ride to the shore of Bataan was terrifying. "Hundreds of bombs—it seemed to us—and right over our heads! We flattened ourselves in the bottom of the boat. The boatsman poured on the gas. We skipped along over the waves with three planes flying low in our wake."

Carlos was lucky—two soldiers on the boat with him were killed by machine gun fire from above. When they reached land, they discovered the dock at Cabcaben had been blown away. Carlos could see sharks in the water; he made it to shore on a makeshift gangplank of bamboo poles.

The beach was a mass of chaos and confusion. In the press of ambulances, trucks, and command cars and honking horns, Carlos searched frantically for the captain who was supposed to meet him with a car to take him to the Bataan airfield. No luck. And no time to wait.

"The Japanese artillery was closing in," said Carlos. "From overhead came the scream of enemy bombers. Far off I could hear the sound of blasting. In the jungle, wherever bombs crashed, new fires sprang up like torches . . . Bataan was in retreat."

A lieutenant with Carlos flagged down a car that had dropped officers by the beach and ordered the driver to take Carlos to the airfield. The driver stared in disbelief, protesting that it wasn't possible to get through. He was commanded to do it anyway.

So, Carlos and the driver inched their way through the swarm of traffic—all coming at them. Theirs was the only car headed the other way. Sometimes Carlos got out to attempt to entangle the car from the jam.

Hours later, they reached the airfield. It seemed deserted. Carlos and the driver went next to the motor pool area, where Carlos knew there was a phone. The phone was dead.

At that moment, an officer appeared. He told them that before communications had gone down, word had been left for Carlos to head to another airfield, at Cabcaben. There, Lieutenant Roland J. Barnick, a pilot, would be waiting for him with a plane—if, of course, the plane hadn't been bombed first!

By now, it was close to midnight. When Carlos and the driver finally reached Cabcaben, shells were dropping over the airfield. But over in a thicket, Carlos spotted a light; they made for it. A group of men was working on a plane hidden under bamboo.

"It was the funniest-looking plane I had ever seen. It looked like something reclaimed from a city dump," said Carlos.

"'Let me make you acquainted,'" said Barnick [the pilot],

'with the Old Duck. We're trying to get her to fly. If we do, okay. If we don't—oh-oh!'"

Getting the dilapidated contraption into the air was a heart-stopping exercise. The motor choked and spluttered; at one point sparks flew and Carlos felt sure the whole thing would explode.

At last, the Old Duck began to hum and they pulled it onto the field. Then they had to wait for the moon to give enough light to take off. It was eighteen minutes after one in the morning when the moon rose over the jungle, still blazing with shells and explosions.

It was now April 9, the day of surrender.

Six men piled into a plane meant for four. There were no seats. "The Old Duck creaked and jerked down the bomb-pitted field," said Carlos. "She managed to lumber into a waddle that carried a little speed. Then she was off the ground—she was over the water—she hung a few inches above Manila Bay.

"Barnick turned in his seat to yell down at me, 'Last man out of Bataan, eh, Colonel!'"

Barnick had never flown a Grumman Duck or any amphibious plane before; he was unfamiliar with the dials and controls. One propeller was stuck, and there were no dashboard lights, so he had to use a flashlight to see anything. They were hit by friendly fire as the plane limped just above the water. Finally, in order to gain altitude, they had to throw out everything—luggage, helmets, even parachutes and pistols. Carlos kept a case with important papers and the letters friends had entrusted to him.

It was a good thing he did.

They were supposed to land in the harbor in Cebu Island, but Japanese antiaircraft fire made that impossible. And they were almost out of gas. However, on an impulse before leaving Corregidor headquarters, Carlos had asked for a map of secret airfields and had slipped it into his case. He consulted that map now, and a little later they landed on an island that had one of them.

After a stop for fuel, they proceeded to another airport in Iloilo. From here, Carlos would eventually head to Australia, and then spend the war years writing and giving public talks about the Philippines in the United States. Like MacArthur, though, Carlos would return. But on this heartbreaking day, he couldn't know that.

After the exhausted travelers had breakfast, they stood on the airfield, listening to a radio over a loudspeaker. Carlos recognized the voice of Norman Reyes, one of his assistants, still in the dusty radio booth on Corregidor, making the Voice of Freedom radio broadcast.

Reyes ended his speech this way: "'Bataan has fallen, but the spirit that made it stand—a beacon to all the freedom-loving peoples of the world—cannot fall!'"

The words were so painful that Carlos turned, as if to run away. To his surprise, Barnick reached out and hugged him. The two men, one American, one Filipino, stood together, tears running down their cheeks.

"And we didn't give a damn who saw us cry."

LAST DAYS ON CORREGIDOR

Japan's military planners had anticipated that the battle for control of the Philippines would take place around Manila, not in the thick, difficult jungles of Bataan. General Masaharu Homma was supposed to have gained a quick victory, then moved Japanese troops to other strategic spots in the Pacific.

Now that Bataan had fallen, Homma was more impatient than ever to end things—and that meant grabbing Corregidor.

After April 9, Homma aimed all his resources at Corregidor, launching ground shelling from guns on Bataan in addition to air attacks. Wooded areas on Corregidor were burned into stumps. The number of wounded soared; patients had to be put into double and triple bunk beds. The power plant providing electricity to the Malinta Tunnel was damaged, and sometimes surgeries had to be performed by flashlight.

The water shortage got worse. It was the dry season, and island reservoirs were depleting rapidly. Each person on Corregidor was allotted only one canteen of water a day—to drink, bathe, and wash clothes.

Corregidor was devastated, one long day at a time. "The beach defenses were demolished, the huge seacoast guns silenced, and the antiaircraft batteries reduced to impotence during these twenty-seven days," wrote Louis Morton. "At the end of the bombardment the island was literally a shambles."

During one attack, army nurse Lucy Wilson was near the mouth of the tunnel when a shell landed. Soldiers eating outside caught the full force of the explosion, with many wounded or killed. Lucy came upon a horrific scene minutes later.

Soon after, Lucy was called to the office of the chief nurse and ordered to be ready to evacuate by submarine later that night: May 3. By this time, though, Lucy was so demoralized and exhausted she wasn't sure she had the strength to go anywhere. She was also extremely underweight—the inadequate diet, long hours of work, and chronic diarrhea had taken their toll.

"I was so sick and tired of retreating, I thought to myself that I wouldn't do it," she said. After leaving the meeting, Lucy happened to share her doubts about evacuating with a patient. Shocked, he burst out, "'Get up and get out of here, now!'"

His words gave Lucy the boost she needed. On the night of May 3, 1942, Lucy, along with a dozen or so other nurses and some army and navy officers, climbed aboard a small boat for a perilous rendezvous with a submarine in Manila Bay. There wouldn't be time or enough submarines available to get all the nurses out; it's likely Lucy's poor physical condition had put her on the list.

"Soon the world was bright with moonlight, shellfire, and bombs. Suddenly a big dark object rose up out of the water in front of us," said Lucy. "They started hurrying us to get on board the submarine *Spearfish*.

"The hatch was such a small opening. Even with my weight only being 70 pounds after the starving, diarrhea, and vomiting over the past five months on Bataan and Corregidor,

I didn't think I would be able to get into it, but I saw other people getting down it, so I did too."

Lucy was in the last group of American nurses to escape capture. Dozens still remained in the Malinta Tunnel. All told, seventy-seven military nurses, sometimes called "the angels of Bataan," were interned as prisoners on the grounds of Santo Tomas University from 1942 until February 1945. These nurses made up the largest group of American women prisoners held during the war.

LUCY WILSON AND DAN JOPLING'S WAR

Army nurse Lucy Wilson Jopling returned to serve in the Pacific after being evacuated from Corregidor.

You can read about Lucy Wilson Jopling's journey on the USS *Spearfish* in my book *Dive!* Lucy made it home, but her ordeal in the Philippines didn't keep her out of action. She volunteered as a flight nurse in January 1944, evacuating wounded soldiers from Pacific battlegrounds, including Guadalcanal, and then going back to the Philippines. Lucy became a veteran at jungle living, enduring engine failures in small planes, harsh living conditions—and lots of bugs, which she began to collect as a hobby.

When Lucy returned to the Philippines in early 1945, she often asked American soldiers if they'd come across her fiancé, Dan Jopling. She heard rumors he'd been killed. In fact, after being captured on Bataan, Dan survived the Bataan Death March and was a POW at Cabanatuan when he was sent to Japan on the *Oryoku Maru*, one of the Japanese transports known as "hell ships."

The ship was attacked in December 1944 by American forces unaware POWs were on board. Dan made it to shore, was recaptured, and then held in camps in Japan and Korea until September 1945. Like other POWs in the Pacific, he endured horrific conditions.

Lucy Wilson and Dan Jopling endured extreme hardships serving their country in World War II. This remarkable couple was reunited and married on December 5, 1945.

This aerial photo shows the Japanese transport *Oryoku Maru* under attack by US planes on December 15, 1944. About 1,600 POWs were crammed in the hold, including Lucy Wilson's future husband, Dan Jopling.

The submarine USS *Queenfish* (not shown) rescuing British and Australian prisoners of war, survivors of the Japanese ship *Rakuyō Maru*, sunk by the USS *Sealion* in September 1944. More than a thousand POWs perished.

After the war, Lucy and Dan married and had four children. Dan worked in public relations for the military, and in the early 1950s he got posted to Japan, where Lucy and their children joined him for two years. Dan died in 1985 and Lucy passed away in 2000.

LEARN MORE: To find out more about Japanese "hell ships," visit Navy History and Heritage Command: https://www.history.navy.mil/browse-by-topic/wars-conflicts-and-operations/world-war-ii/1944/oryoku-maru.html.

Help for PTSD: During World War II, thousands of POWs like Dan Jopling endured brutal physical conditions and atrocities; the physical and emotional effects of these experience often followed soldiers throughout their postwar lives. In her memoir, Lucy Wilson Jopling wrote, "War is Hell. I don't care which one or where . . . and you *never* forget it!"

Today we understand more about PTSD, or post-traumatic stress disorder, a mental health condition that can affect military veterans or anyone who has suffered a physical or emotional trauma.

The National Center for PTSD is a program of the US Department of Veterans Affairs that provides assistance and education to individuals and families impacted by PTSD. If you or someone you know is struggling with upsetting memories, difficulty sleeping, or feelings of depression and anxiety after a traumatic event, there are effective treatments. Do speak with a trusted adult. You can also share this US Department of Veterans Affairs website: https://www.ptsd.va.gov/index.asp.

Surrender on Corregidor—May 6, 1942

Lucy Wilson left the Rock on May 3—just in time. A final enemy assault on May 5 damaged nearly all the American guns serving as beach defenses. That night, a lookout spotted Japanese troops coming ashore. The Americans put up resistance. Between six hundred and eight hundred men were killed and a thousand more wounded.

General Jonathan Wainwright made his decision the next morning; delaying surrender would cost lives—and wouldn't change the outcome. Wainwright ordered the American flag

Japanese landing craft approach Corregidor.

lowered and destroyed so it wouldn't fall into enemy hands. A white flag took its place.

Wainwright sent a surrender message to General Masaharu Homma, and then he alerted President Roosevelt and General MacArthur: "'With profound regret and with continued pride in my gallant troops, I go to meet the Japanese commander.'"

Battalion surgeon Ralph Hibbs was now helping patients at Hospital #1 on Bataan. For the time being, at least, Japanese officials were leaving the hospital undisturbed. (As we'll see later, the hospital's medical staff and patients were moved to a prison in June.)

And so from his vantage point just a few miles away on Bataan, Ralph had witnessed the attacks on Corregidor during its last days. He saw the end.

"By noon on 6th of May, a quiet crept over the tadpole-shaped rock," he said. "The smoke settled. Corregidor had fallen. A white flag flew atop the flag pole. Then it was replaced by the rising sun."

The flag of Japan now flapped in the breeze.

A Japanese war photo showing captured Allied troops on Corregidor outside of the Malinta Tunnel.

"We surrendered only when further resistance became impossible."

—Sam Grashio, fighter pilot

Cabanatuan prison camp.

Drawing of Cabanatuan Camp by Ben Steele.

PART 2

ENDURANCE AND RESISTANCE

Spring 1942–Fall 1944

"Gone are the hopes of joy to come,

And home again to see,

Gone is the wish to carry on

And add to the misery.

Starvation's grim and ghastly hand

Has stricken body and mind

Until each black and weeping night

Leaves fewer ghosts behind."

—Dr. Ralph W. Hubbard
Liberated POW of Cabanatuan,
from a poem written in prison camp

Captured soldiers under guard at the start of the Bataan Death March.

THE BATAAN DEATH MARCH

EYEWITNESSES: HANK COWAN, ED DYESS, SAM GRASHIO

It's time to circle back and pick up Hank Cowan's story on April 9, when Bataan fell, and find out what happened to Hank and other soldiers after the surrender. A day earlier, an officer had instructed Hank's unit to make their way to the town of Mariveles on the tip of Bataan. It took Hank and the others all night to walk there.

Soon they heard that General Ned King had officially surrendered the American and Philippine forces under his command. Hank was told to put down his weapon and wait in a large open field with other soldiers. No one knew what would happen next.

"I had taken my rifle and broken it over a rock. I had a wrist watch, a large sheath knife, and my wallet, which I put under a large stone," said Hank. "I was determined they would get nothing from me."

This Japanese war photo shows captured troops after the fall of Bataan. Soldiers like Hank Cowan sat in the hot sun for hours with no food or water before being forced to march sixty-five miles north to the town of San Fernando with little water or food.

Japanese guards began searching prisoners for souvenirs and weapons. Word got around: Don't be caught with anything made in Japan. Japanese soldiers assumed these items had been taken from a dead comrade and would retaliate with a beating—or worse.

"We were held in this open field for about 24 hours," Hank said. "Then we were ordered to move out to the road and start walking. Most of us had not had anything to eat or drink for at least a day and we were getting hungry and thirsty."

Food and water were scarce in the days to come. Random beatings and brutal actions were frequent. "The Battle of Bataan had cost the Japanese a lot, slowing up their timetable of conquest and costing them thousands of soldiers," Hank reflected later.

"They started taking revenge right away. Every time we passed a truck load of soldiers they would bang us on the head with sticks and rifle butts. It was lucky that most of us had our GI helmets. It was humiliating to us to be treated

Soldiers on the Bataan Death March.

like this. This was just a sample of what we were to endure later."

Hank knew the enemy wanted the prisoners out of the way; POWs were pushed to move as fast as they could go. The Japanese were preparing for their final assault on Corregidor, just offshore, and were bringing in artillery weapons to this part of Bataan.

"As we walked by our little air strip at Cabcaben, we saw the Japanese setting up gun batteries and firing on Corregidor," Hank said.

Carlos Romulo had escaped from the pockmarked Cabcaben airfield in the Old Duck in the early morning hours of April 9. Now it was in enemy hands.

"They marched us without rest, giving us no food or water. They changed guards every three hours so they were already fresh. Our men, already weak from short rations and disease, soon began to fall out of the column," Hank said.

"The Japanese wasted no time with stragglers; they were either shot or run through with a bayonet. Soon the sides of the road were littered with dead men. This had become a march of death for the men that had fought so gallantly for America and the Philippines."

The brutal treatment didn't let up. "The heat was terrible and men risked their lives for a sip of the vile, scum-covered water in the ditches alongside the road. I stumbled along, my mind blurring, not caring whether I lived or died," said Hank.

"We marched for what seemed an eternity. Still we were not allowed to stop for water ... I was beginning to get so

THE BATAAN DEATH MARCH

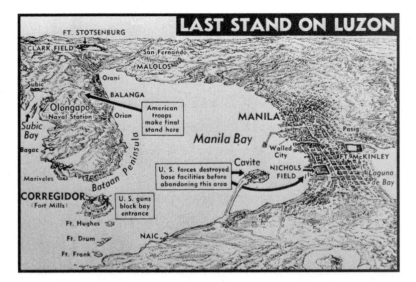

Here's the map of Luzon again, so you can see the route. The grueling sixty-five mile Bataan Death March skirted the southern tip of the peninsula, then hugged the eastern edge of Bataan, bringing the prisoners north through Orion, Balanga, Orani, and then east to San Fernando.

tired I knew I could not go much further. There were sugar cane fields along the road and many men were killed trying to get a stalk of the cane to chew on."

At one point, Hank ran into a field to pick a stalk of sugar cane, fully expecting to be shot. He got back to the column safely, but fell behind the others. Stragglers were often killed, but this time a strange thing happened. A guard grabbed his arm and helped Hank catch up: a rare act of kindness. Hank clutched his sugar cane stalk and kept chewing it to get a little energy.

Hank's searing memories bring to life a horrific chapter in World War II history: the Bataan Death March. The march was not one long, continuous column of soldiers. Rather, it consisted of different groups of a hundred or so men. Not all groups left at the same time and each survivor's experiences were slightly different. For instance, after cook Ruben Flores was captured near Hospital #1, he was put to work by his captors for several days before joining up with the march.

Most soldiers, though, began the deadly march in Mariveles, on the western tip of the Bataan Peninsula, and walked to San Fernando, visible at the top center of the map on the previous page. There they were loaded on trains to travel twenty-five miles to Capas. The last stage was to walk about nine miles more to Camp O'Donnell, formerly a military training center now being used as a POW camp.

Military historian Sidney Falk detailed some of the factors that contributed to the horrors of the march. "The Bataan Death March and its bitter aftermath were the result of four tragic conditions: the extremely weak physical state of the American and Filipino troops when they surrendered, the unpreparedness of the victorious Japanese to receive them, the contempt in which Japan's military held its prisoners, and the cruelty and callousness of the average Japanese soldier."

The Japanese were ill prepared to care for the large numbers of American and Filipino soldiers they had captured. They also didn't anticipate the Allied soldiers' extremely poor physical condition. Many were weak and malnourished from months of reduced rations. Allied soldiers were also suffering from tropical diseases like malaria, dengue, and dysentery. During the march, in addition to random killings by guards, many Filipino and American soldiers died of their illnesses and also from heatstroke.

The viciousness and violence of the Bataan Death March unfolded mile by mile, carried out by individual Japanese soldiers or units. Guards also used torture techniques such as "sun treatment," where prisoners were forced to sit for hours with no head coverings in the blazing heat.

While his defenders later argued that General Masaharu Homma wasn't aware of the barbarous actions of those under his command during the Bataan Death March, he was held responsible. Homma was executed in 1946 for war crimes committed under his watch. There's evidence that another Japanese officer, Colonel Masanobu Tsuji, who eluded capture and trial for alleged involvement in atrocities in Shanghai and in the Philippines, encouraged the mistreatment and execution of prisoners on the march.

What emerges in account after account of survivors is the sheer brutality of the Japanese guards. Allied prisoners who tried to stop along the way to drink water from ditches were punished; exhausted soldiers were forced to sit in the sun; there was very little food or water; men were struck and killed for minor offenses or trying to help others. Filipino citizens who stepped forward to aid the marchers were punished or chased away.

It's clear that many of the deaths during the Bataan Death March could have been avoided. During the surrender negotiations in April, General Ned King had tried to press the issue of his men's welfare with his Japanese counterpart. King had pointed out that American trucks could be used to transport captured soldiers out of Bataan. His pleas went unheeded.

Exhausted soldiers on the Bataan Death March.

Precise numbers of those who marched and died are unknown, though most historians estimate that about 75,000 soldiers surrendered on Bataan, a figure that included somewhere between 10,000–11,800 Americans. A historical report from the Department of Defense estimated that between 7,000 and 10,000 Filipinos and approximately 600 Americans died on the march.

The tragic deaths of those who had fought so hard on Bataan didn't end once the march was completed. As we'll soon see, things got even worse once the prisoners reached Camp O'Donnell.

Many accounts by American soldiers of the atrocities

committed during the Bataan Death March were written or recounted in oral histories years later. But in January 1944, the first inkling of the fate of soldiers after the defeat on Bataan reached a shocked American public.

The account was written by someone we've already met here: pilot Ed Dyess, who was part of a daring escape from a prison camp in the Philippines in 1943 and returned home to the United States to tell his story. Ed's memories of the Bataan Death March were vivid; he could easily recall the details of events he'd so recently endured.

"At 3 a.m. of April 12, 1942—the second day after our surrender—we arrived half dead at Orani, in northeastern Bataan, after a twenty-one hour march from Cabcaben near the peninsula's southern tip," Ed wrote. "That thirty-mile hike over rough and congested roads had lasted almost from dawn to dawn.

"It would have been an ordeal for well men," said Ed, who marveled that they'd made it even that far. "We had had no food in days. Chronic exhaustion seemed to have possessed us. Many were sick. I know men who could never remember arriving at Orani. They were like Zombies—the walking dead of the Caribbean."

Unlike Ed, fellow pilot Sam Grashio wrote about the Death March forty years later, when some details had faded. "The March was a macabre litany of heat, dust, starvation, thirst, flies, filth, stench, murder, torture, corpses, and whole brutality that numbs the memory . . ." he said.

"While I remember many individual incidents on the hellish Death March, I cannot recall their sequence in any but the most general way."

However, Sam did recall that he often stuck close to Ed, whom he admired and respected. Sam recalled that, perhaps because Ed was over six feet tall, he was often a target for harassment.

At one point, a guard knocked off Ed's helmet. "He then gave Ed a fierce beating and kicked him into a ditch," Sam recalled. "I made a halting gesture to come to Ed's aid and for my pains was kicked back into the ranks."

The six days and nights of the Bataan Death March had seemed like an eternity to Hank Cowan. At last, when he

Death March survivor Ben Steele captured the brutal treatment of prisoners on the Death March in this postwar illustration.

and his group reached the town of San Fernando, they were allowed to rest and given a little rice and water.

"As we departed for our first P.O.W. camp the next day," Hank said, "little did we know this horrible nightmare was only beginning. At San Fernando we were stuffed into little box cars for the final journey to Camp O'Donnell . . .

"But if we had known what lay ahead, most of us would have preferred to have died on the march."

Prisoners' March
(Death of a Friend)
by Lt. Henry G. Lee

So you are dead. The easy words contain
No sense of loss, no sorrow, no despair.
Thus hunger, thirst, fatigue, combine to drain
All feeling from our hearts. The endless glare,
The brutal heat, anesthetize the mind.
I cannot mourn you now. I lift my load,
The suffering column moves. I leave behind
Only another corpse, behind the road.

CAMP O'DONNELL: DEATH AT THE END OF THE MARCH

EYEWITNESSES: ED DYESS, SAM GRASHIO, HANK COWAN

When Ed Dyess first saw five old boxcars waiting at the railroad siding at San Fernando, he figured each might hold fifty men. But at least one hundred soldiers were forced into one car with him. Then the door was locked from the outside for the journey to Capas.

"There was no room to move. We stood jammed together because there wasn't sufficient floor space to permit sitting," Ed remembered. "As the day wore on and the sun climbed higher the heat inside the boxcars grew to oven-like intensity. It was so hot that the air we breathed seemed to scorch our throats."

Many soldiers were suffering from dysentery, a severe intestinal infection that causes cramps and bloody diarrhea. "The atmosphere was foul beyond description. Men began to faint. Some went down from weakness," Ed continued. "They lay at our feet, face down in the filth that covered the floor boards."

Ed's friend Sam Grashio remembered the stink being so overwhelming he felt as if he were suffocating. To make matters worse, Sam was in horrible pain. During the march, a guard had struck him with a bamboo stick. The blow had split his mouth and broken a tooth.

"My broken tooth throbbed constantly," Sam said. "Some of the [train] cars had steel sides. These became fearsomely hot, veritable sweat boxes. It took about four hours to negotiate the twenty-five miles [to Capas] but most of the men were so overwhelmed by the heat and stench and so cramped that they had little sense of either time or movement."

That was certainly the case for Ed. "Later I heard that a number of men had died in each of the five cars," he said. "I don't know. I was too far gone to notice much at the journey's end."

At last the train stopped at Capas, a town in Tarlac province. The final leg of the Death March was a walk of about nine miles to Camp O'Donnell, the former Philippine army training camp the Japanese had decided to use to house prisoners. Concerned Filipino civilians continued to line the road, but guards tried to prevent them from giving the prisoners food or water. Some people tossed offerings to the marching men anyway, and ran off before guards could stop them.

"As we straggled on we had ample reason to bless the kindly Filipinos of Capas," Ed recalled. "Having seen other prisoners pass that way, they had set out cans of water among the bushes and in high grass along the road."

The guards kicked over most of the cans. "But some were overlooked and a few of us were able to take the edge off our thirst," Ed said. "One gaunt American officer said he believed he owed his life to the good and thoughtful townfolk of Capas."

Ed got his first look at O'Donnell from the top of a rise about a mile away. "I saw a forbidding maze of tumbledown buildings, barb wire entanglements, and high guard towers," said Ed. "I had flown over this dismal spot several times, but never had given it more than passing appraisal.

"I wondered as I looked at it now how long I would be there; how long I could last."

For many American soldiers, Camp O'Donnell would be the first of several prison camps, including Cabanatuan and labor camps in Japan and Korea. Other soldiers, both American and Filipino, would never leave O'Donnell alive.

"When we had been at O'Donnell about a week, the daily death rate among the Americans was twenty a day," said Ed. "Filipinos were dying at a rate of 150 a day. In two weeks fifty Americans were dying each day. The Filipino death toll had soared to 350 each twenty-four hours.

"Many new prisoners arrived daily," he continued. By the

A burial detail at Camp O'Donnell, where thousands of Filipino and American soldiers perished from disease and malnutrition. Men were buried just outside the main gate; another cemetery had to be added to deal with the horrific death toll.

end of April, the last group of prisoners from the Bataan Death March had arrived in the camp. "Most of them were sick and all were in varying stages of starvation. The disintegrating building that passed as a hospital soon was packed. Men were laid shoulder to shoulder on the bare floor. There were no blankets. Many of the sick and dying were naked."

The flies were unbearable. And there were "flies by the millions," Ed said. "They droned all day long, settling alternately upon the filth, then upon the containers of gray rice.

"Starvation was everywhere. Men who had weighed two hundred pounds or so now weighed ninety or less. Every rib was visible. They were living skeletons, without buttocks or muscle. On seeing a man lying asleep it was difficult to say whether he was alive or dead."

Men at Camp O'Donnell died of malaria, dysentery, and from tropical diseases such as beriberi, which is caused by a deficiency of vitamin B1, or thiamine. One symptom of the deficiency is swelling, and Ed saw fellow prisoners with feet, ankles, and legs swollen to twice their normal size.

Most of the POWs had at least one affliction, especially malaria, which is spread by mosquitoes. And no wonder. "Mosquitoes descended upon us in clouds," said Ed. "Few of the prisoners had blankets, mosquito nets, or any other protection."

Despite all this, Ed looked back on this time and realized he and his men hadn't given up. "It may seem ridiculous, but in the face of all our adversities, we continued hopeful and optimistic during the first month of captivity," he said. "Indeed, there were many of us who never despaired of regaining our freedom, even though hope after hope was blighted."

Before the surrender, Japanese officials had inspected both O'Donnell and Cabanatuan, another former Filipino army training camp about forty-five miles away, and concluded the two would be sufficient to hold an anticipated twenty-five thousand prisoners.

But O'Donnell was vastly inadequate for the more than fifty thousand men who arrived in the spring of 1942. The crowded conditions, lack of sanitation, inadequate medical treatment, and inhumane treatment by guards combined to make Camp O'Donnell one of the deadliest POW camps in history.

Although exact numbers are impossible to determine, an American POW who worked in the camp commandment's office later said he recorded as many as thirty thousand deaths within a few months, including more than twenty-seven thousand Filipino soldiers and more than seventeen hundred American soldiers and civilians who worked for the military.

The Department of Defense's historical report on deaths at Camp O'Donnell reports similar figures, estimating that over fifteen hundred Americans, or one out of every six men, and twenty-six thousand Filipinos died in the spring of 1942. Some experts put O'Donnell's death rate for POWs at 30 percent, compared with three percent for military prisoners held by the Nazis. (This figure only applies to enemy prisoners of war. Nazi concentration camps and killing centers in Europe resulted in the state-sanctioned murder of more than six million Jews.)

Soldiers like Hank Cowan didn't need statistics. They could see the horrors of what the prisoners called "Camp O'Death" with their own eyes. "The buildings were soon filled to overflowing and many men had to crawl under the floors of the buildings to escape the torrents of monsoon rains," Hank recalled.

"This was where I slept. Shortly after we arrived, the Filipinos were separated from the Americans and we had no further association with them." A road separated the two sections of the camp; the American prisoners were kept in the smaller section.

The guards selected some prisoners for forced work details around the islands. But the inadequate food rations made physical work difficult. The diet, Hank decided, "was designed to slowly starve us and remove any resistance we might have had. The water supply in camp was short and we barely had enough drinking water to go around. There was none for washing and laundry.

"Sanitary conditions deteriorated fast and by the end of the first month dysentery had reached epidemic proportions. Many men had contracted the disease from drinking contaminated water from the ditches on the Death March. Open latrines and lack of sanitation made the camp a perfect breeding place for the disease.

"Of all the diseases to plague the weakened, confined men, dysentery was without a doubt the worst. It caused terrible pain, uncontrollable diarrhea, and vomiting. It turned men into skin and bones almost overnight," said Hank. "The disease literally ate up the intestinal tract and caused a horrible death. The death rate rose to the point where the able-bodied men could not bury the dead fast enough."

Dysentery was a painful, horrific way to die. In the heat, patients wore nothing but a small covering. Most were unable to stand to use a bucket or latrine. The high death rates led to the Japanese decision in May to release the remaining Filipino prisoners back into their home communities and begin moving the American POWs to Cabanatuan.

Prisoners at Camp O'Donnell in May 1942.

By this time, Hank was deathly sick with malaria and dysentery; he burned with fever and was wracked by chills. "God only knows why I did not die there like the others. Maybe it was a blessing that my mind became blurred by the disease. I do not know if I could have endured the suffering. There was a long period of time when my mind was almost a blank," he said.

Hank was so sick that the journey to Cabanatuan, about thirty-six miles to the east and sixty miles north of Manila, was mostly a blur. He recalled being in the back of a truck. "I saw the trees along the road and wanted to lie under a cool tree and die. I probably would have jumped if my buddies had not restrained me.

"The next thing I remember was lying on a dirt floor in a building with dying men all around me, and the ever present smell of dysentery. I was sure I must be dying and I wanted to talk to someone that would tell my folks what had happened to me. I seem to remember talking to someone, but it could have been my imagination. The man lying next to me was dead and a blanket covered his body.

"I took the blanket and covered myself. Then my mind was blank again."

Hank had come to Cabanatuan.

REMEMBERING CAMP O'DONNELL

We met photographer Carl Mydans briefly in Part One, when he and his wife, Shelly Smith Mydans, were captured in Manila in January 1942. When American forces landed in the Philippines in late 1944, Carl returned, too, on an assignment to take photos for *Life* magazine. In early 1945, he accompanied American soldiers to the long-abandoned Camp O'Donnell.

What he found there helps us imagine the terrible story of the camp that historian John C. McManus has called "the Andersonville of the Pacific," after the notorious Civil War prisoner of war camp in Georgia. (The Andersonville National Historical Site is also the home of the National POW Museum. You'll find a link to their website in the Resources to Explore section.)

Today, the Capas National Shrine on the site of the former camp includes a grove of trees, a wall listing the Filipino soldiers who died, a tall memorial obelisk, and a small museum that includes one of the boxcars into which POWs were packed for the journey from San Fernando to the town of Capas. Here is Carl's description of what he saw there in early 1945.

Carl Mydans: Camp O'Donnell's Silent Story

"In other camps we would enter, flaccid men would come toward us with impoverished bodies and sluggish minds and talk and talk about what had happened to them," Carl began. "In its lonely desolation, Camp O'Donnell told its story silently, in the long rows of empty prison shacks with crumbling roofs of nipa [palm] leaves, the empty sentry boxes standing awry, the broken fences with barbed wire falling away and trailing along the ground like vines.

"Thick grass had grown up around the last reminders of the men of Bataan who had lived and died there: a canteen worn to a pearly finish by those who had held and shared it through those months of fighting and of starvation; a tin dinner plate, dented and discolored; an army mess pan . . . piles of rusting tin cans, heaps of rags; bits of frayed rope ends; a worn and broken wooden leg with decaying straw fastenings; a pile of fire-stained rocks cradling a charred and rusted helmet where dying men once cooked weeds and grass. All over the ground and in the tumbling shacks they lay, talking to us wherever we found them.

"And all about, stretching off into the quiet fields, were the graves: mass graves under unmarked mounds and hillocks of earth; acres of others marked with crosses made of sticks, overgrown, all but obliterated, some with dog tags nailed to them, some with names carved lovingly by comrades. I knelt before one to read an inscription. 'Good-by,' someone had carved upon it. 'We will always remember you.'

"By the time we liberated Camp O'Donnell that was the most we could do: remember."

A view of the Cabanatuan prison camp (originally designated as Camp #1). This became the main facility used to house American POWs in the Philippines. It was located approximately nine kilometers (about five-and-a-half miles) from the city of Cabanatuan.

Another nearby site, called Camp #2, was used briefly in the spring of 1942 but closed because of water issues. Camp #3, east of Camp #2, was in use from the end of May until October 1942, when prisoners were transferred to the main POW camp.

At one time, Cabanatuan held as many as ten thousand men. Over the course of the war, groups of prisoners were transferred out for work details in the Philippines or transported to labor camps in Japan. Once Americans returned to the Philippines in the fall of 1944, the Japanese transferred nearly all the remaining Cabanatuan prisoners to Japan on ships, leaving only about five hundred.

FROM CAMP O'DONNELL TO CABANATUAN

EYEWITNESSES: ED DYESS, HANK COWAN, RALPH HIBBS

A ny place, we thought, would be better than O'Donnell," said pilot Ed Dyess. "So we looked forward to Cabanatuan camp, which was to be our new home, according to the guards."

Ed was moved to Cabanatuan in June, after two months at Camp O'Donnell. The guards said his group would be traveling by truck, but the men would have to carry anyone unable to walk to a loading area outside Camp O'Donnell.

When he set out on foot, Ed had his doubts that the promised trucks would actually appear. "As we passed through the gates and into the hot highway I figured that we were on another death march and that we would lose about half our several hundred men."

A photo from Cabanatuan shows George Muller, left, who was so tall he had trouble finding shoes to fit his large feet. A note with the photo says he fought barefoot at times.

Prisoners at Cabanatuan were forced to watch Japanese propaganda films. The man on the right is carrying a bench in preparation for a showing. The original photo caption indicates this road was dubbed "5th Avenue" by the POWs.

But to his surprise, trucks did arrive: American-made ones at that—Fords, Chevrolets, and GMCs. The prisoners were packed in so tightly they couldn't move. "We didn't care, however," said Ed. "We were riding."

The trucks made the prisoners hopeful their lot might improve. "We probably wouldn't have been so cheerful if we had known what was in store for us at Cabanatuan," Ed said. "After two and one-half hours of jolting and jogging we were there."

When Ed's truck rolled into Cabanatuan, he counted three large compounds for prisoners surrounded by barbed wire and guard towers equipped with machine guns.

"Prisoners from Bataan and Corregidor already were there when we arrived. They had named all roads and trails that connected the three compounds. There were Broadway, Market street, Michigan avenue, Main street and many others.

"A Milwaukee man had named a path for himself," Ed said. "It was Buboltz boulevard and led to the latrines."

Though sometimes called Camp Pangatian, after a smaller town close by, Ed's new camp was commonly known as Cabanatuan, after a larger city about five and a half miles to the east. It was located about forty-six miles north of Camp O'Donnell in central Luzon. (Although in the spring of 1942 Allied prisoners of war were held in three separate locations, as noted earlier the largest, Camp #1, soon became the main prison encampment for POWs.)

Cabanatuan prison camp was surrounded by grasses and rice paddies, with only a few trees. The open landscape offered guards on the towers a good view of the surrounding area. Once used as a training center for the Philippine Army, the camp contained more than a hundred barracks in parallel rows. There was bunk space for about eight thousand prisoners. The men slept on bamboo slats, which were uneven and hard, but adding straw was just an invitation for unwanted bugs.

A hand-drawn map of the camp in a book of POW writings shows that the Japanese area of the camp had barracks,

Cabanatuan prison camp with thatched roof barracks and tables in background.

storage facilities, a garage, a baseball field, a carabao (water buffalo) corral, and, surprisingly, a pond for ducks and geese.

The poultry proved easy prey for the ingenuity of hungry men. Dr. Ralph Hibbs (we'll follow his journey to Cabanatuan a bit later) recalled that before they were caught, POWs managed to widen the wire mesh between the prisoners and the pond enclosure to "goose size, allowing the little quacky morsels into our area.

"The capture was painfully slow, painstaking, and dangerous. It required complete silence while using highly technical equipment [a hook made from a pin on a line]. It was difficult but necessary to be out of sight during the entire heist. Also complete riddance of the feathers was mandatory." It worked, for a while. Ralph guessed that about half a flock of forty had disappeared before the guards caught on.

Many Bataan survivors, including Ed Dyess, Sam Grashio, and Hank Cowan, came to Cabanatuan from O'Donnell in May and June 1942. Others, like Dr. Ralph Hibbs, spent months in Bilibid Prison in Manila before being transferred to Cabanatuan in December 1942. By the time Ralph arrived, fences had been reinforced and strengthened. There were three barbed wire perimeter fences. The inner one slanted sharply inward, making escape impossible.

To maintain order within the camp, the American POWs organized themselves in military fashion. While there were some civilians and servicemen of other nationalities at Cabanatuan, most prisoners were American soldiers still on active duty.

At the outset, the highest-ranking field officer, Lieutenant Colonel Curtis Beecher, assumed command; Lieutenant Colonel James Gillespie took charge of the hospital. Neither was there when the camp was liberated in 1945. Gillespie had died of dysentery. Beecher was put on the hell ship *Oryoku Maru* in December 1944; he survived camps in Japan and Korea before being freed in September 1945.

The Cabanatuan hospital included thirty wards built to hold forty patients, though often the number of men in each ward was twice that. Dysentery patients were in a separate quarantine area, and within that section was a special ward for the sickest patients, nicknamed Zero Ward, because once soldiers entered, their chances of survival were close to zero.

Hank Cowan knew all about Zero Ward. When he came from O'Donnell to Cabanatuan, that's where he ended up. Hank recalled that there were actually two wards for the worst cases. "I found out later that they were called Zero Ward and St. Peter's Ward, both of which had been set aside for the extremely sick and dying men. Indeed, St. Peter's Ward was more like a morgue than a place for the living, and Zero Ward, where I was, was little better.

"Every morning the dead were gathered up and taken to a shallow mass grave. By the next day the torrents of monsoon rain would have washed away the soil revealing parts of the dead men."

It took Hank a long time to get better. His memories of this time were heartbreaking, traumatic, and impossible to forget. He suffered constantly, as did the men all around him.

Hank called them "living skeletons with dysentery eating their guts out, maggots working in their rectums.

"The American medics did what they could for them but sometimes cried in frustration because they had nothing to work with. I do not know why I remained alive after all this time."

At one point, Hank was given a small portion of condensed milk along with his meager rice ration. "This must have saved my life, for I came out of my stupor and began to see my surroundings. I gained strength slowly and came to see what a terrible state I was in. My coveralls had not been removed since Bataan. All body eliminations had gone into them. My beard and hair were down to my shoulders and were matted and full of lice."

Slowly, Hank cleaned himself as best he could, and found someone with a pair of scissors who cut his hair close to his head. "Someone brought me a pan of water and as I washed my head I left a layer of squirming lice on the water," said Hank.

He would live. His memories would live also. "The burying detail that left each day with naked, emaciated bodies was something I can never forget."

200TH COAST ARTILLERY AND NEW MEXICO

Lorenzo Banegas from San Ysidro, New Mexico, knew all about Zero Ward. At Cabanatuan, Lorenzo contracted diphtheria, a serious bacterial infection now preventable by a vaccine.

Working in the Cabanatuan fields, his symptoms grew worse. Lorenzo said, "'The diphtheria caused my feet to swell up, my tongue swelled and there was pus on top of [my] mouth. I couldn't swallow so I gave my ration of rice to my friend.'"

He was taken to Zero Ward. "'They called it the "Zero Ward" because zero percent would come back. When I got sent there, they hugged me like I wasn't coming back.'" Eventually, Lorenzo got better and tried to cheer up other patients.

Lorenzo was one of about eighteen hundred soldiers from the New Mexico National Guard who had undergone training in the US before being activated as the 200th Coast Artillery regiment in the Philippines in September 1941. (A second unit, the 515th, was formed from it; soldiers in both groups helped to cover the retreat of soldiers into Bataan at the start of the war.)

According to the New Mexico History Museum, the state paid a high price: More than eight hundred of these soldiers perished in the Philippines. Each year, the Bataan Memorial Death March is held at the White Sands Missile Range to honor these and all victims of the march.

Some of the regiment members were Latino and fluent in Spanish, and veterans' oral histories show how these young men, some of whom knew each other from home, supported one another. While at Cabanatuan, Lorenzo composed a fourteen-verse song in Spanish in the tradition of Mexican folk songs entitled "Corrido de Bataan."

This 1990 photo shows Jimmy Lopez, founder and director of the New Mexico National Guard Heritage Museum (now the New Mexico Military Museum). Lopez was a National Guardsman in the 200th Coast Artillery and survivor of the Bataan Death March and POW camps. He founded the museum to commemorate the history of the National Guard in New Mexico and to honor the sacrifices of those who fought in Bataan.

"'Ruben Flores [see Chapter Three] and I still sing that corrido together,'" Lorenzo later said. At Cabanatuan "'We used a guitar that somebody made using caribao guts for strings.'"

Lorenzo's song was included in a Latinos Initiatives exhibit at the Smithsonian in February 2002, but unfortunately, Lorenzo passed away on December 15, 2002, at the age of eighty-three. His good friend Ruben Flores died in April of the same year, at age eighty-four.

To watch interviews with Lorenzo Banegas and Ruben Flores speaking about their wartime experiences, follow links in the Resources to Explore section. Their interviews and others are part of the Veterans History Project, American Folklife Center, Library of Congress.

You can read about the experiences and challenges faced during World War II by Latino soldiers and veterans at the National Park Service website in an essay by Lorena Oropeza entitled "Latinos in World War II: Fighting on Two Fronts, Proving Valor in War, Seeking Equality at Home," https://www.nps.gov/articles/latinoww2.htm.

CABANATUAN: RATS, RICE, AND LICE

EYEWITNESSES: SAM GRASHIO, ED DYESS, HANK COWAN, RALPH HIBBS

T he main activity of everyone in camp who was not dead or wishing himself dead was trying to get more food," said pilot Sam Grashio. Desperation drove Cabanatuan prisoners to extremes. "If someone was sick or about to die, others stayed close to him, less from compassion than from hope of getting his rice ration."

Sam had been lucky not to fall ill during his two months at Camp O'Donnell or at Cabanatuan in the summer of 1942. Nevertheless, he was always extremely weak from the subsistence diet.

"The basic trouble was simply that there was not enough of anything. Consequently, everyone lost weight at an appalling rate," he said. "My normal weight was about 135, but I was once reduced to an 85 pound skeleton."

Rice was the main staple. It was served three times a day, sometimes with mongo beans or camotes, a kind of sweet potato. But prisoners simply weren't getting enough protein or vitamin C. Sam said, "It was a diet that barely kept one from starving to death."

Starvation could make men desperate. If there were worms in the rice, the POWs ate the meal anyway. And there was a constant search for more food. Besides stealing and eating the guards' poultry flock, "Anything that ran, swam, flew, or crawled was captured and eaten: monkeys, iguanas, dogs, cats, frogs, lizards, rats, snakes, worms, weevils, grasshoppers, and snails," Sam said.

A Christmas religious gathering at Cabanatuan in December 1943. The photo was taken by Major Paul Wing with camera and film bought on the black market and smuggled into camp. Japanese guards did allow chaplains to hold religious services. Sam Grashio, who was Catholic, credited the chaplains and his strong faith with helping him survive.

"So was much that was inanimate: animal entrails, fish heads, decaying vegetables, flowers, weeds, and any root that could be chewed."

When asked why he never ate rats, one POW said, "'I didn't catch any—somebody always seemed to beat me to them.'"

Especially after he was first captured, Ed Dyess talked, thought, and dreamed of food constantly. "At first I wanted steaks; big Herford steaks from Shackelford county, Texas. Then my fancy settled upon eggs. I wanted them fried and by the platter.

"Each night as I lay down to sleep I was tortured by this craving. I dreamed of them. Sometimes it seemed I was wallowing in gargantuan plates of eggs, smashing the yellows and absorbing them through my pores.

"As it always is in dreams, I never could taste or smell the eggs. Invariably I awakened, madder than hell and hungrier than before."

At Cabanatuan, Ed noted, there was an active black market with items Japanese soldiers bought from local people and then sold for exorbitant prices within the camp. Ed had managed to bring money with him when he was captured by hiding it inside his socks—between his toes. "It was in fairly large bills and while it rubbed blisters and sometimes made walking painful, I held on to it."

Ed remembered that prices were extremely high, especially at first. "There was hardly an item—such as tinned fish, bar candy, or cigarettes—that didn't sell for five dollars."

A prisoner at Cabanatuan with barracks and prisoner gardens in the background. Photos from inside the camp are rare.

The black market was also the inspiration for a dish the prisoners developed called "quan," mentioned in several POW survivor accounts. The expression may have come from the word kwan in Tagalog, which has no direct translation but can be applied to almost anything. According to Ed, "We used it to designate such extra food as we could get by fair means or otherwise."

Hank Cowan explained that most of the POWs not in the hospital managed to get a quan pot, a large can with smaller cans inside. "Charcoal was salvaged from the main camp kitchen, and when put in the bottom of the large can which had holes for a draft, the small can acted as the cooking pot when it was set on the hot coals inside the large can," he said. "Anything we could scrounge or steal was cooked in this manner."

Ed described using a tin bucket for the same purpose. His recipe for quan was as follows: "Obtain from the black market or commissary a small can of fish and some coconut lard. At chow time get a mess kit filled with rice. After lining a 'quan' bucket with lard, put the rice along with some wild red peppers you have managed to gather while on jungle detail.

"The bucket then goes into a bed of hot coals and the food in it bakes. We thought it mighty fine, but if I never see any more of it, it will be all right with me."

As for where the POWs ate, Ed explained that in the beginning some men had taken food to their barracks to eat there, but they soon gave it up. "The rice drew flies which, like most undesirable mealtime guests, remained the rest of the day. So we took to squatting in the open to dine.

"This started talk about the probability that we wouldn't know how to act at splendid functions after the war. We wouldn't be able to balance teacups and salad plates on our knees or handle the table silver of civilization," said Ed. "We decided that when food was served we would take our salads and teacups into a corner and eat like a pack of wolves. This would be taken by our hostess as (1) our peculiar whimsy or (2) would so startle her and the other guests that there would be no comment."

Sadly, the charismatic pilot didn't get many chances to put this black humor scenario to the test. He left Cabanatuan in October 1942, after guards announced a call for men to move to other camps. There were rumors that some would be sent not to Japan but to another POW camp, the Davao Penal

Colony on Mindanao Island. Both Ed Dyess and Sam Grashio decided to take a chance and volunteered.

"I didn't want to go to Japan, where there would be no chance of escape, but I was so sick of Cabanatuan I would have been willing to go almost anywhere," said Ed.

Once again, Ed had made the right call. The following April, Ed and Sam were part of a group of ten Americans and two Filipinos who engineered a remarkable escape from Davao. Sam remained on Mindanao as part of guerrilla operations until he was rescued by the USS *Bowfin* submarine on September 29, 1943. A few months earlier, Ed and two others also escaped by submarine. Their rescue was arranged by guerrilla fighters in radio contact with General Douglas MacArthur's headquarters in Australia.

Once back in the United States, Ed recovered his health in the hospital and was able to share his story with military officials and the *Chicago Tribune* newspaper, which was eager to publish Ed's account of the Bataan Death March. However, the War Department delayed permission for four months.

Ed's extraordinary story, the first news the American public had about the Bataan Death March, finally appeared in January 1944. It created a sensation, but the brave pilot wasn't alive to see or enjoy the publication of his memoir. Ed had returned to active duty and was killed in a training accident in California on December 22, 1943, at the age of twenty-seven. Although it appeared Ed had a chance to escape from his fighter plane, he instead guided it into a vacant lot to avoid civilian casualties.

Ed Dyess has not been forgotten, however. Dyess Air Force Base near Abilene, Texas, is named in his memory.

While Ed Dyess and Sam Grashio were at Cabanatuan for just a few months in 1942, Hank Cowan spent the rest of his war there. And getting enough to eat remained a constant struggle, helped only by the rare arrival of Red Cross packages.

"So many men died the first year that the Japanese increased our diet and gave us some more rice and some water buffalo meat and seaweed soup," said Hank. "This slowed the death rate but a lot of men were just too far gone for it to do any good."

Eventually, Hank was well enough to leave the hospital ward and was assigned to duty in the camp's vegetable gardens. "What a relief it was to get away from the sick and dying and be able to do something. We got the water system in the camp working and even rigged up a shower, which was a blessing for us all."

Determined to stay alive, Hank came up with an ingenious way to get more food while working in the main camp garden. The guards took most of the vegetables for themselves and would beat prisoners caught with any produce when returning from work details. Hank found a way around that.

"I acquired a large pair of pants and a hat with a high crown. When I went to work, I tied the legs around my ankles and let the legs bag down. I had holes in the pockets and I would put small vegetables in them and they would fall down the legs to the tie around my ankles. I also put vegetables in the crown of my hat," said Hank.

Chopping wood at Cabanatuan.

When Hank was searched, a guard would slap at his pockets but then let him go. "If I had been caught it would have meant a terrible beating, or they might have even broken my arms."

Along with the inadequate diet, bugs were an ongoing issue. "When we first came to Cabanatuan the lice were very bad," Hank recalled. "Then someone brought in bed bugs, and they must have killed or run the lice off because they disappeared. The bed bugs were worse, however; they tried to get what little blood we had left. There was just no way to get rid of them."

The firsthand accounts of POW survivors like Hank put a human face on the grim statistics of POWs in the Pacific during World War II. Efforts to treat prisoners of war humanely were first launched in the nineteenth century by Henri Dunant, founder of the International Red Cross. He proposed that countries sign international agreements setting forth guidelines for humane treatment. The representatives of thirteen nations met in Geneva, Switzerland, in 1864 and signed the first Geneva Convention, which protected medical staff, the wounded, and prisoners of war.

However, although Japan signed the Geneva Convention of 1929, the nation didn't ratify it. And while Japan stated in 1942 that it would follow the rules for humane treatment, the evidence and survivor testimonies demonstrate extreme violations.

According to the National World War II Museum, "More than 27,465 Americans captured in the Pacific fell outside of the protections of the Geneva Conventions in relation to prisoners of war. The death rate among POWs in the Pacific was over 40 percent—11,107 would not return home. Most of those who perished were starved to death, ravaged by tropical diseases, or were killed while being transported in the holds of unmarked vessels termed 'hellships.'"

A feature on POWs for the Corporation for Public Broadcasting series *American Experience* notes, "That Japanese forces did not strictly follow the Geneva Conventions is hardly a matter of debate. According to Dr. William Skelton III, who produced a document entitled *American Ex-Prisoners of War* for the US Department of Veterans' Affairs, more POWs died at the hands of the Japanese in the Pacific theater and specifically in the Philippines than in any other conflict to date.

"In Germany in WWII, POWs died at a rate of 1.2%. In the Pacific theater the rate was 37%. In the Philippines, POWs died at a rate of 40%. In total 11,107 American soldiers captured in the Philippines died. Some died in the Philippines. Others were transported and died in places like Korea, Taiwan, Manchuria, or the Japanese home islands. Still others were killed in the 'Hell Ships' en route to Japan, ships that were bombed by American planes or torpedoed by American ships whose crewmen did not realize their countrymen were in the transport holds."

Prison camp survivors like Hank Cowan bore eyewitness testimony to atrocities committed on the Bataan Death March and at Camp O'Donnell and Cabanatuan prison camp. Along with health problems resulting from their ordeals, many POWs carried the emotional trauma and scars for the rest of their lives.

"Beatings became so common most of us just took them as a matter of course. I guess the worst beating I had was for eating a sweet potato in the field," said Hank. "The guard hit me in the hip with the butt of his rifle. I got an egg-sized knot from that one that hurt for months and even bothers me today. It was a wonder I was not shot."

Hank went on, "In a prison camp you live from day to day, endure the ridicule and beatings, and have faith that the next day will bring something better or decide to give up and die.

"As time goes by, you pray and hope."

SURVIVING CABANATUAN—ODDS AND ENDS OF LIFE IN CAMP

MAIL

"Mail was distributed to us only three times in the three years of our imprisonment," said Dr. Ralph Hibbs. The first time was August 13, 1943. Ralph received a letter from a college friend that had come through the International Red Cross in Switzerland. It was dated nine months earlier. Another man that same day fainted after receiving a letter that his mother had died.

A POW named George Distell sent a Red Cross form letter to Henry Ford, the automaker. He actually received a response—from Mr. Ford's secretary. (His other notes, to entertainers Jack Benny and Bob Hope, weren't answered.)

CABANATUAN FLAG, AKA TP

Dr. Ralph Hibbs credited a marine sergeant named Jim Costello with inventing the "Cabanatuan flag," a solution to the lack of toilet paper. The flag was cloth tied to a short stick. After use, it was rinsed and hung up until needed again. Ralph said the outside barrack walls were decorated with Cabanatuan flags fluttering in the breeze.

The Cabanatuan orchestra.

THE BAND

Although it took a long time for the band to get permission, Corporal Johnny Kratz and his "Rice Balls" eventually performed a weekly concert for the enjoyment of their fellow prisoners. (Ralph Hibbs mentions in his memoir that he never knew where the band members got the instruments.) Tragically, Ralph reported that all except one member were lost on a hell ship en route to Japan.

MORE ON RATS

Ralph also reported on the rat situation, including the time a mess sergeant demanded that no more rats should be cooked in his kitchen. (The cooking of rats continued to take place secretly.)

Once, Ralph spotted "a truly remarkable sight—four dressed rats evenly arranged on a metal platter," all ready to be popped into a fire pit oven. "My reaction was only disappointment at not being invited to their gourmet meal," he said.

"TELL MacARTHUR TO WAIT"

Ralph often played chess at Cabanatuan with a set carved from carabao horn. He recalled an incident when someone stuck his head through the open door and joked, "'MacArthur just rolled up in a tank.'

"With my eyes glued on the board, contemplating the next move of my bishop, I replied, 'Tell MacArthur to wait.' It had been just too damn long. Almost three years. Most everybody was dead. Nobody gives a damn. The chess game seemed about as important as fighting a war."

Ralph later entitled his 1986 memoir *Tell MacArthur To Wait*. In it, he reported that playing chess every day in prison camp made him a pretty decent player. Returning home, he beat his mom in a game of chess in five moves—and she was the champ of her local club.

An Execution
by Lt. Henry G. Lee

Red in the eastern sun, before he died
We saw his glinting hair; his arms were tied.
There by his lonely form, ugly and grim,
We saw an open grave, waiting for him.
We watched him from our fence,
in silent throng,
Each with the fervent prayer
'God make him strong.'
They offered him a smoke; he'd not have that.
Then at his captor's feet coldly he spat.
He faced the leaden hail, his eyes were bare;
We saw the tropic rays glint in his hair.
What matter why he stood facing the gun?
We saw a nation's pride there in the sun.

OF RICE AND MEN: POW WRITERS AND POETS

Along with language lessons, photography, and musical performances, the prisoners wrote and created art about their experiences.

This poem and several others here are the work of Lieutenant Henry G. Lee. A survivor of the Bataan Death March, Henry began writing poetry in notebooks he kept in Cabanatuan prison camp, noting that, "'The best I can say of the majority of these poems is that they are true as I could make them; the worst, that they are not written by a talented nor experienced poet.'"

In 1946, while still recovering after the war, Major Calvin E. Chunn, who was at Cabanatuan and then held in Japan, compiled prisoners' work recovered from Cabanatuan prison into a book entitled *Of Rice and Men*. This rare volume is now long out of print.

(I managed to find a used copy after searching a long time. It's autographed by Major Chunn himself. When I open it, that signature helps connect me to the men who lived through experiences I can only imagine.)

In the book, Calvin Chunn explains that before Henry Lee was sent to Japan in December 1944 on the *Oryoku Maru*, he wrapped his poetry notebooks in canvas and denim and buried them under his barrack at Cabanatuan. Other POWs who contributed to *Of Rice and Men* also buried their work before being sent to Japan.

Henry survived the sinking of the *Oryoku Maru*, but was put on another ship. Henry and several hundred other POWs were killed in early January 1945 in Formosa when US planes bombed the *Enoura Maru*.

Calvin explains that one of the Signal Corps photographers with the Sixth Rangers, who liberated Cabanatuan on January 30, 1945, returned to the camp to dig up the notebooks. Dr. Ralph Hibbs reported that intelligence officers also returned to recover death and hospital records buried in jars.

Calvin Chunn himself (1915–1983) survived a prison camp in Japan and was liberated in Korea. Calvin went on to have a successful career in public relations and journalism.

RALPH AND PILAR: BILIBID TO CABANATUAN

EYEWITNESS: RALPH HIBBS

It's time to loop back and catch up with what happened to battalion surgeon Dr. Ralph Hibbs before he came to Cabanatuan.

Ralph was still on Bataan helping patients at Hospital #1 when Corregidor fell on May 6, 1942. He was spared the ordeal of the Bataan Death March and the horrific conditions at Camp O'Donnell. For a while, the hospital and medical staff were left alone, but after the fall of Corregidor, things began to change.

"They put troops into our area and informed us we should ready ourselves to evacuate the patients on short notice," said Ralph. He'd heard rumors about the conditions at Camp O'Donnell, so when Ralph learned he'd be sent to Bilibid

Captured soldiers from Corregidor Island arriving at Bilibid Prison in Manila in May 1942.

Prison in Manila he was relieved. "Again my luck was holding out. The reports from Bilibid, although meager, pictured a more stable and livable prison."

On June 24, 1942, Japanese soldiers pulled up in rickety old trucks. "They allowed us to take nothing from the hospital," said Ralph. "I threw my first-aid kit and scruffy rucksack over my shoulder and climbed onto a truck filled with patients."

Ralph couldn't know what lay before him, but he felt ready. "There was a certain relief on leaving the blood-soaked miserable peninsula where we had bled and fought for some six months.

"This disease-ridden, infested, smelly piece of mountainous jungle and burial ground had been a place of suffering, starvation, and fear of unlimited proportions. The bleak hopelessness was well left behind. The future in prison camp, we reasoned, will just have to take care of itself."

On the way to Manila, the trucks stopped at a village for water and Ralph was allowed to get out and fill his canteen.

In this February 1945 photo, emaciated POWs liberated by American forces from Bilibid Prison in Manila are given a meal. POWs at all camps in the Philippines suffered from malnutrition.

Local citizens appeared and gave him some rice balls. They beckoned him behind a *báhay*, a type of stilt house in the Philippines, and urged Ralph to escape into the hills. At that moment, no guards were in sight.

Ralph was tempted. He knew the guards hadn't gotten an accurate count of the American prisoners; he probably wouldn't be missed. He also knew some American soldiers had fled into the jungle to fight as guerrillas. His heart pounded as he weighed his choices. But in the end Ralph decided to take his chance in prison. Ralph was a doctor first and foremost. And his skills might well be needed in a prison camp.

Ralph returned to the group and climbed back into the truck. Many times in the terrible days ahead, he would wonder if he'd made the right decision.

In June 1942, when Ralph arrived at Bilibid in Manila, it

was six months from when he'd said a rushed goodbye to his girlfriend, Pilar Campos. Back then, he'd urged her, "'Don't get mixed up in this mess.'"

But of course, Pilar had, as Ralph was soon to find out. She wasn't alone. From guerrilla fighters to members of the underground resistance, to individuals risking their own lives to step forward to offer food to American and Filipino prisoners on the Bataan Death March, the people of the Philippines resisted their nation's occupation by Japan.

Journalist Carlos Romulo noted, "The Filipinos, as a people, did not yield to the Japanese. Civilian resistance went on from the moment the first Japanese flag went up on Philippine soil."

Bilibid Prison had been built in 1898 and was just that: a prison complex, with stone buildings. "My assigned space was in the old three story former hospital building, so I took refuge on the third floor with a few fellow officers," said Ralph. "The desk clerk assured me it had a nice view—huge wide open window—at least over the wall."

That window would prove to be important.

To his surprise, Ralph found he was able to sleep well on the concrete slab that passed for a bed. He thought his body was probably trying to make up for so many sleepless nights on Bataan. He also reflected on the changes he'd gone through—from dating Pilar Campos in peacetime, to desperately fighting to save lives in the jungle, and now, to being a prisoner of war.

"It was amazing. One could go from a sharkskin dinner jacket to no shirt and tattered pants, and from an innerspring mattress to a bed of rock in six months."

One day, a Japanese guard fetched Ralph and brought him to a small waiting room. There Ralph found a Catholic priest who told him, "'Ralph, Pilar asked me to come and visit you. In January she heard you were killed.'"

Somehow, though, Pilar had managed to get more recent news of Ralph. The priest, Theodore Buttenbruch, known to all as Father Ted, had brought a note from Pilar and some money. Ralph would have to hide it, but money in prison camp was useful. It could purchase extra food on the black market. At times, local vendors were allowed in to Bilibid to sell bananas or sometimes breadfruit, salt, or soybeans. An ounce of salt cost one American dollar.

Father Ted then whispered that Pilar had been riding her bike outside the prison's north wall at 2:00 p.m. each day, hoping to see Ralph and make contact. "The next day I anxiously waited for Pilar to come by," he said. "I paced back and forth like a groom before his wedding, peering out of the large, open window of the third floor. My bedraggled, dirty outfit consisting of a sleeveless shirt and khaki shorts partially filled by a skinny carcass presented an unromantic figure.

"After several unrecognizable people went by riding bicycles, I saw Pilar. My heart jumped—what a thrill!"

Pilar wore a floppy straw hat to hide her face and made no sign she'd seen him, but Ralph imagined her peeking out from

This March 1945 photo of Bilibid, taken after the prison was liberated by American forces, shows where prisoners were buried near a wall. American POWs from Corregidor and medical personnel, including Dr. Ralph Hibbs, spent time at Bilibid, built as a prison in 1898.

under it. A bit later, he spotted her sitting with some friends on the porch of a house up the block. This time she did wave!

"I felt warm inside as my morale soared. Then she was gone," said Ralph. But what if guards noticed her hanging around and became suspicious?

"There were aftershocks with the realization that Pilar was getting mixed up in this mess. She was a brave girl."

Two weeks later, Father Ted came to visit again. This time he brought a note from Pilar, along with a small packet she'd asked him to smuggle in to Ralph: money, vitamins, and a medal of St. Christopher, patron saint of travelers. Pilar had also sent another gift: three small bananas to be hidden under Ralph's shirt.

"'I'll try to see you again,'" Father Ted told Ralph, but the priest couldn't make any promises, saying, "'It's getting very difficult.'"

Ralph didn't meet the priest again, but he never forgot Father Ted's soft, twinkling gray eyes. A church biography honoring Father Ted Buttenbruch explains that since he was originally from Germany (an Axis nation aligned with Japan and Italy), the priest initially had some freedom to visit prisoners and bring food and medicine to Allied prisoners of war.

That freedom didn't last. Father Ted's underground activities soon brought him to the attention of the Japanese authorities. He was twice imprisoned and accused of espionage. It's believed he was tortured and executed by the Japanese sometime in late 1944.

But even without Father Ted, Pilar managed to find another contact to smuggle in more vitamins and money to Ralph. The couple also derived a secret communication system. When Ralph caught sight of Pilar riding by on her bicycle, he'd attach a note to a rock and heave it from the third floor out to the street, trying to aim it close enough that she could nonchalantly stop and scoop it up.

"The first time the rock rolled in front of her bike it startled her since she had no warning of my scheme," said Ralph. "She ignored it and then after some ten minutes came back and picked it up. This worked successfully six or seven times during my stay at Bilibid." They were never caught.

One night, Ralph and Pilar were even able to touch hands through an opening in the wall near a drainage pipe. Pilar passed him money, medicine, and vitamins. Later, Ralph lay on the concrete floor, smiling to himself at Pilar's bravery and loyalty.

Through the grapevine, Ralph learned that despite the poor diet at Bilibid, conditions at his prison were a thousand times better than O'Donnell. For one thing, Bilibid had flush toilets. He also heard that Camp O'Donnell was being closed, with the Filipino prisoners released back into their communities, in a sort of parole.

And like most other American POWs, Ralph would be sent to Cabanatuan. That fall, Ralph wrote to Pilar to tell her the news. "'I'd rather stay here where at least I can see you. Thanks for the help. I'm really OK and not worried other than for your safety. Please take to the hills. Love you—R.'"

Cabanatuan was about a hundred miles away, and Ralph didn't expect to see Pilar once he was there.

He underestimated her determination.

On the day of departure, Ralph and other prisoners rode in open trucks to the railroad station. They journeyed to Cabanatuan by train and then on foot.

"Our next stop: Cabanatuan. A cruel POW camp and uncertain future lay ahead," Ralph wrote later. "As we plodded along sweltering in the tropical sun, motivated by the glistening bayonets of the guards, I decided not to look too far ahead or I might stumble on my own boots."

On December 10, 1942, Ralph got his first sight of the prison camp where he would stay for more than two years, until he was rescued on January 30, 1945.

Prisoners tried to organize life at Cabanatuan by making gardens of their own, forming a band, and writing poetry. When not helping patients, Dr. Ralph Hibbs played chess and bridge, and took a class in Spanish from another prisoner. The wartime caption of this 1942 photo indicates that the man in it is West Point graduate Major James S. Neary, who was later sent to Japan, where he died in February 1945.

Like other POWs, Ralph found the crowded barrack huts uncomfortable. The thatched roofs did a poor job of keeping out seasonal rains. The bamboo slats for sleeping made for a hard, uncomfortable bed.

But there had also been improvements during the previous few months. By the time Ralph arrived, American prisoners had the camp well organized. The medical team ran a hospital and three clinics throughout the compound and did their best with scarce equipment and medicine.

Ralph realized almost immediately there was little chance of escape. Along with the fences, guards were always on duty. "Guard towers manned by two soldiers with rifles and a machine gun were mounted at each corner and midpoint on each side of the fence. The odds clearly favored the victors, and left no sport for us in trying to escape," said Ralph.

In addition, the guards had devised extreme measures to deter POWs from making a run for freedom. The prisoners were put into groups of ten and told that if one man in the group tried to escape, the other nine would be shot. After being forced to watch the execution of men who tried to escape, the men in Ralph's group decided it was simply not worth the risk.

Ralph had also witnessed the torture meted out to three men caught bringing sacks of food into camp. All three were killed in extremely brutal ways. Those searing images stayed with Ralph the rest of his life.

Writing more than forty years later, he reflected, "Their only crime was trying to help others . . . I vowed that if I survived, I would help everyone that I possibly could. Torture or revenge was never an ingredient in my plans."

Ralph found it wasn't easy to be a doctor at Cabanatuan. "Prison life for a medical man was a never-ending witness to the cumulative effects of starvation," he said. "The ration was always below starvation level. The extra foods we received from time to time made survival possible."

Ralph encountered diseases he'd only read about in textbooks. He treated scurvy, caused by a deficiency of vitamin C; eye problems as a result of a lack of vitamin A; and beriberi, brought on by a deficit of vitamin B1. It was frustrating to be without the medicine or equipment he needed, and to be weak and underweight himself. At one point he weighed 120 pounds rather than his usual 178. Ralph said, "Everything happening in camp related to agony, cruelty, and dying."

The young physician could never really get used to the horrible condition of his fellow POWs. "Those walking around presented a picture of emaciation or a bloating beyond recognition. The paths of camp were usually empty except at messtime, since no one had the strength to waste," Ralph observed.

Recalling the nickname of the soldiers fighting on Bataan, he continued, "The battling bastards of Bataan became a grave picture of hideous suffering and neglect, ravaged by a savage captor. It was nothing if not the most depressing scene I'd ever seen. Even the landscape of our camp seemed naked, as colorless as its inmates."

Despite this, Ralph and the other medical men worked as hard as they could to ease the suffering around them. After the count of prisoners in the morning, Ralph headed to the hospital barracks.

When Ralph first arrived, dysentery was rampant. "On several mornings men would be found lying at the entrance stairs, too weak to walk and rocked with excruciating abdominal cramps," he remembered. "They had crawled to a hospital barracks, the natural place to seek relief. They stared vacantly at the misery around them until death spared them further suffering."

At first, it didn't seem that much could be done to keep the disease from spreading. Men contracted dysentery, often caused by bacteria from the poor sanitation in open latrines, and from consuming contaminated food or water. Soap was hard to come by and it was almost impossible to keep fingers and hands clean.

"Agonizing abdominal cramps and retching would seize the victim and in a few days his strength would be gone and he would be too," said Ralph. "The sufferers could not make the trip to the latrine. Victims would lay down close to the latrine and die . . .

"Something had to be done."

An American officer named Major Emmet C. Lentz came to the rescue. Lentz had been trained in military medicine, and he developed a rudimentary but innovative septic tank and latrine system to improve camp hygiene.

Lentz used metal from a long-abandoned automobile in the corner of the camp to construct a metal trough, which was put on an incline. From this he fashioned a makeshift handmade septic tank, and used a fifty-gallon drum of water to wash waste from a ten-seat wooden "throne," latrines positioned at the top of a small incline. His invention reduced contamination and disease.

Ralph said it simply, "It saved the camp—it made it livable."

In June 1943, about six months after Ralph arrived in camp, he volunteered to take charge of the tuberculosis (TB) ward. "The tuberculosis ward of about forty patients became my responsibility and my love from 8 June, 1943 to January, 1945. It turned out to be a real challenge which I readily accepted."

Tuberculosis is a lung disease caused by bacteria, and since it can be spread when someone sneezes or coughs, Ralph's job was to isolate the infected men. Patients with TB were exempt from work details, and visiting the ward was forbidden.

Ralph had no medicine; however, the camp hospital had acquired a microscope, which made diagnosing cases possible. With little to work with, Ralph did his best to keep his patients alive.

Ralph didn't know it when he began, but his role as the doctor of the TB ward might have helped to save his own life too.

Physicians like Ralph performed wonders in the makeshift camp hospital. They sometimes did simple procedures without anesthesia. In severe cases of malaria, the doctors crushed quinine tablets and injected them intravenously. Guava leaf tea was used to treat diarrhea.

Once, the medical staff performed an emergency appendectomy. Later, in September 1944, when a US plane mistakenly shot at the camp striking a prisoner, a surgeon performed an emergency leg amputation that saved the man's life.

Ralph remembered that military dentists in camp filled cavities with metal by grinding silver coins. And teeth from carabao, a domestic local water buffalo, were shaped to fill the gap of a missing tooth.

While Ralph spent his days treating patients, other prisoners were sent on various work details, such as laboring in the camp gardens, chopping wood, and driving trucks under guard to bring in supplies from town. The truck drivers were the main source of information about news of the war and the outside world.

And that's how Ralph learned that soon after he left Manila, Pilar Campos had been arrested and imprisoned for trying to pass food to American POWs being transported in a truck. Pilar was released, but the incident brought her to the attention of the Kenpeitai (sometimes spelled Kempeitai in English), the military police arm of the Japanese army, similar to the Gestapo in Germany.

Undeterred, Pilar and other young women organized a group called the Volunteer Social Aid Committee. Their true purpose was to aid American POWs. But to cover up their underground activities, Pilar and her friends devised a creative cover story.

They put together a singing and dancing program and cultivated friendships with Japanese officers in Manila, learning some basic Japanese. The young women then offered to come to Cabanatuan to entertain the Japanese guards and administrative command.

The ploy worked. On September 24, 1943, Ralph received a secret message from a POW who'd returned from a wood gathering detail outside camp. Ralph learned that Pilar and seven other young women would visit Cabanatuan the following day. He watched for them, positioning himself on the main camp road. They rode past in an open truck. Pilar was ready. Spotting Ralph, she tossed him a small package of medicine and vitamins.

Ralph's friends had also arranged for him to pretend to work backstage as the young women performed. "I looked up and there was Pilar, singing not over two meters away. She was beautiful."

The two weren't able to speak. Ralph never saw Pilar again. She continued her resistance activities, with tragic consequences. In February 1945, when American and Japanese troops were engaged in fierce fighting for control of Manila, Pilar was brutally killed by Japanese soldiers. Her mother, brother, and some of the civilians she'd been shielding in their home were also murdered.

Ralph learned that earlier, the Campos home had been searched by Japanese intelligence officers. They found the army footlocker with his name stenciled on it—the footlocker Pilar had brought from his apartment for safekeeping. It clearly linked her with an American.

Even after being imprisoned once, Pilar had not stopped her resistance activities or her efforts to smuggle food into camps for American POWs. Because of her association with Americans and underground activities, the family was marked as enemies of the emperor. On the day she died, Pilar stood up to Japanese soldiers, who shot and then bayoneted her.

Years after the war, Ralph, along with friends of Pilar, launched an effort to honor her. On May 13, 1983, a presidential Certificate of Appreciation was presented to surviving relatives in Manila to recognize Pilar's heroic efforts to aid American prisoners of war.

WOMEN IN THE PHILIPPINE UNDERGROUND

Along with Pilar Campos and Claire Phillips, other women active in the Philippine underground included Margaret Doolin "Miss U" Utinsky, an American-born nurse married to a POW who did not survive. Utinsky assumed a Lithuanian identity and hid from the Japanese to avoid being interned when foreign nationals were captured in early 1942. She was active in an underground network to smuggle in food, medicine, and money to Allied POWs.

Before the war, the Philippines had opened its doors to Jewish refugees from Europe. Japan was an ally of Nazi Germany, which perpetuated systematic atrocities against Jews in Europe in the Holocaust. However, the Japanese did not target Jewish families living in the Philippines. For that reason, a Jewish refugee from Vienna, Austria, named Hanna Kaunitz remained free in Manila during the Japanese occupation. Unlike American civilians, she and her family were not interned as they were considered citizens of Japan's ally.

Taking advantage of this, both Hanna and her brother became active in the Philippine underground. Like Pilar, Hanna began dating an American physician who became a prisoner of war at Cabanatuan and later in Japan. However, unlike Pilar and Ralph, this romance had a happy ending.

After the war, Hanna Kaunitz married Dr. Albert Weinstein and they moved to Atlanta, Georgia, where they raised their family.

The Philippine underground was active throughout the occupation. Here, an unidentified woman stands in front of the Tsubaki (*tsubaki* is Japanese for *camellia*) Club, opened and run in Manila by singer Claire "High Pockets" Fuentes Phillips. The club was a place to make contact with members of the Japanese military to obtain information to pass on to guerrilla fighters.

Claire Phillips, code name "High Pockets," with daughter, Dian. Claire entertained high-ranking Japanese military officers and passed on information to the Allied underground and guerrillas.

In this famous photo of the landing on Leyte Island on October 20, 1944, General Douglas MacArthur is shown fulfilling his 1942 promise to return to the Philippines. American troops landed on Luzon Island (where Manila and Cabanatuan are located) on January 9, 1945.

PART 3

RACE
AGAINST
DEATH

Fall 1944–Winter 1945

WE HAVE RETURNED

We first met journalist Carlos Romulo in Part One. Carlos wrote *I Saw the Fall of the Philippines* in 1943, during the war, while he served an ailing President Manuel Quezon, also in exile in the United States. (The version of his book I obtained is a first edition, with passages censored, or blacked out, by the War Department.)

Carlos returned to the Philippines with General MacArthur in October 1944, and was an eyewitness to the triumphant landing in Leyte, an island south of Luzon. The following passages are drawn from his companion memoir, *I See the Philippines Rise* (1946).

"Surrounding our troopship, that morning in Leyte Bay, were six hundred other American ships, troop carriers, battleships, destroyers, cruisers, and rocket ships carrying two hundred and fifty thousand men; a massed unit of Pacific power that had at one time, on our way to Leyte, covered a thousand miles of sea. Overhead the sky was a shield of planes jutting fire . . .

"Home! After two and a half years I felt under my feet again the blood-drenched earth of the Philippines. The land itself raged with fire set by rockets and flame throwers, and all around us was death. Beyond this offensive of ours, we knew, beyond the Japanese lines, Filipinos were fighting and dying, the guerrilla forces that were in this fight to help recover this palm-studded strip of Philippine earth . . . Beyond that smoke and flame were my people, soldiers and civilians, fighting our fight, a valiant, organized, loyal army like none other in the world . . .

"In that moment of landing I remembered something I had pledged myself to remember during two and a half years of waiting. I remembered our Bataan dead who had been left unmarked, unburied, and unavenged. I remembered them as I saw the American flag flying from a coconut tree, and beside it our own Filipino flag with its red and blue and its sun and three stars . . .

"MacArthur, speaking now on Leyte Beach, recalled his pledge, over our hastily set up broadcasting station, the Voice of Freedom: 'We have returned . . .'

"This stretch of bloodied sand was the first mile of the road back.

"MacArthur had spoken the truth. We had indeed come home."

—Carlos Romulo

Led by the USS *Pennsylvania*, repaired after being damaged in the December 1941 attack on Pearl Harbor, a convoy of US ships approaches Lingayen Gulf on Luzon on January 9, 1945.

FALL 1944: NEW HOPES, NEW FEARS

EYEWITNESSES: HANK COWAN, RALPH HIBBS

Late in 1944 there were a lot of rumors that American forces were near," said Hank Cowan. Maybe the tide of war had turned. Maybe General Douglas MacArthur would finally fulfill his promise to return. Maybe the long ordeal of the POWs in Cabanatuan camp would come to an end.

"But there was no concrete evidence," Hank continued. "Our enemy still acted the same as always and their propaganda paper always claimed they were winning. After so long a time even their propaganda was almost believable.

"Our hopes were at a low ebb."

Dr. Ralph Hibbs felt the same. "This camp was like a never-ending road going on and on curving around the mountain, through the valley, searching for home around the next bend but never finding it. Here I saw the wretched, smelled the dead, and heard the dying.

"One year, then two years, and more to come had been squandered in this hell hole. This was no sentence or it would have had an end," he said. "Death is more certain than the end of captivity. It ends the hopelessness of this life. Would freedom or death overtake us? I wondered."

And then, one day, the normal routine changed. The guards didn't show up to take Hank and other prisoners to their garden work detail. With an unexpected day off, Hank decided to rest in the hammock he'd made for himself in the upper part of the barracks, away from bedbugs.

Suddenly he heard the sound of a large formation of planes. Hank had grown accustomed to enemy planes buzzing over Cabanatuan. But these were different. A few prisoners went out to look, but Hank didn't bother at first. He couldn't really believe they might be American. The planes flew on, but when they returned a short time later, Hank did look.

"The moment I saw the formation I knew it was not Japanese," he said. "It consisted of heavy dive bombers in perfect formation and fast little fighter ships circling the large formation. What a beautiful sight!"

Ralph noticed the American planes that day too. Like Hank, at first he couldn't quite believe his eyes. He couldn't bear to get his hopes up either. Then he saw one of the American planes attack an enemy plane, sending it spiraling out of the sky.

"A huge roar went up from inside the camp," Ralph remembered. "Goose bumps appeared. My whole body shook. I was finally convinced. Someone was on our side."

That fall, the prisoners saw more friendly aircraft and dogfights between American and Japanese planes. Sometimes bombs fell on the road or the airfield near the prison camp.

"The sound of the guns and bombs furnished a constant serenade for us and our morale was very high," said Hank. "Finally our guards admitted that Americans had landed on Leyte Island and a terrific battle was in progress. We knew then if we were not murdered by the Japanese we would soon be free."

While the presence of American planes brought hope, there were fears too. "After this first American bombing, rumors circulated that the Japanese intended to execute all remaining POWs," Ralph said.

Ralph wasn't sure whether to believe these rumors, but nevertheless he began to concoct an escape plan. He studied where he could run and looked for ditches in which to hide should guards turn on the prisoners.

Along with the American planes overhead, the men in camp witnessed other changes that fall. Large groups of prisoners were shipped off from Cabanatuan to Bilibid Prison and then to Japan, forced to travel under brutal conditions in the holds of ill-fated hell ships like the *Oryoku Maru*. Ralph guessed that at least three groups of two thousand left the camp that autumn.

"Hundreds of my best friends, officers and enlisted men, marched out the wood-framed barbwire front gate never to be seen alive again," said Ralph.

Once, as some of his companions were taken away, Ralph lingered at the gate until he was shoved with the butt of a guard's rifle. He wasn't sure which fate was more perilous: to be in that large group or be left behind with five hundred others.

"I wondered what was in store for us."

The remaining prisoners at Cabanatuan had good reason to fear. On December 14, 1944, 139 American POWs were massacred at a small prison camp on Palawan, another Philippine island.

Two years earlier, these same Palawan prisoners had been at Cabanatuan. In July 1942, an interpreter and guard at Cabanatuan had announced a call for strong men willing to undertake a special work project lasting about three months. These were similar to other calls for work details. With malnutrition and dysentery rampant in the camp at the time, three hundred men signed up, thinking their chances might be better elsewhere.

Their final destination was Palawan Island, a mostly undeveloped narrow island southwest of Luzon. The American prisoners spent three years there doing hard labor. They tackled the monumental task of clearing land and paving an airplane runway using mostly hand tools and wheelbarrows. In September 1944, the group was divided into two companies; half the men were taken by boat to Manila, leaving one hundred and fifty prisoners on Palawan.

In December 1944, as Japanese commanders conducted surveillance on the movement of American ships and planes, they concluded that a US landing on Palawan could be coming anytime.

Although he later denied giving the direct order to kill the prisoners, Lieutenant General Seiichi Terada, whose responsibilities included Palawan, was later sentenced to life in prison for his part in the massacre of POWs. Whatever the details of the Japanese chain of command and decision process, what happened there was undeniable—and unthinkably atrocious.

At two in the morning on December 14, 1944, all one hundred and fifty POWs were awakened and told to take shelter

The trenches visible near the fence served as bomb shelters on Palawan Island. Guards ordered 150 prisoners into them for a false air raid, then poured in gasoline and set the men on fire. Eleven POWs managed to escape, fleeing down the cliff to the sea, then seeking help from guerrillas.

for an air raid. They were herded into the makeshift bomb shelters they'd already dug. Buckets of gasoline were dumped into the entrances and set on fire. Only eleven men escaped to bear witness to the atrocity.

If this could happen at Palawan, it could happen at Cabanatuan too. At least, that's what one American guerrilla leader thought.

His name was Robert Lapham.

Like thousands of others, Bob Lapham had been fighting on Bataan back in late 1941 and the winter of 1942. But, rather than surrender, Bob had escaped to become a guerrilla leader. And when Americans forces finally returned, he knew exactly what he wanted to tell them.

The POWs at Cabanatuan must be rescued. Before another massacre.

Before it was too late.

POWs IN DANGER

Eyewitness: Bob Lapham

The plight of the prisoners there [at Cabanatuan] had been on my mind for many months," said Robert Lapham. "How many had passed through the gates of Cabanatuan altogether or how many were still alive there, nobody knew for sure."

Guerrilla resistance in the Philippines is a fascinating and complex story all on its own. And while the guerrilla movement is outside the scope of our focus, Bob Lapham does belong here. Bob, along with another guerrilla leader, Lieutenant Colonel Bernard L. Anderson, played a critical role in urging General Walter Krueger to approve the rescue mission soon after American troops landed on Luzon in January 1945. And two of Bob's most experienced captains were essential to the rescue.

Bob first became involved in guerrilla warfare in January 1942 while serving under Major Claude A. Thorp on Bataan. Thorp had received direct permission from General MacArthur to conduct guerrilla-type operations. Thorp and his men sabotaged enemy supply trucks and worked at gathering intelligence, such as discovering the schedule of enemy planes departing from Clark Field to better allow Allied troops to prepare for Japanese bombing raids.

When surrender became inevitable, Thorp gave his men a choice. They could turn themselves in, stay with him, or strike out on their own. Bob decided to form his own guerrilla group and was eager to enlist anyone, American or Filipino, willing

Guerrilla leader Robert Lapham in early 1945. When the photo appeared in American newspapers, he joked that it made him a celebrity for a day, especially when a hometown newspaper in Iowa called him a "Hollywood-style cowboy."

to risk their lives in the Luzon countryside—now, of course, controlled by the enemy.

While some guerrilla units favored hiding out in the remote mountains, Bob set up his base camp in Umingan, a town about seventy miles north of Cabanatuan. Bob reasoned that food and supplies would be easier to get in this more populated area—the lowlands made travel easier than in the mountains—and he was also able to develop trusted relationships with local citizens who could serve as eyes and ears for the guerrilla fighters.

Right away, Bob met several farmers and shopkeepers ready to join him. "Training or no, they were all willing, even eager, to risk their lives to badger the Japanese invaders, and they all assured me that they knew at least ten or fifteen others who would join us and bring rifles with them," said Bob.

"I simply could not turn away men so obviously loyal, courageous, and eager to do something," said Bob. "Within a couple of days I had about twenty-five men and rifles."

These recruits became the nucleus of the Luzon Guerrilla Armed Forces, or LGAF, a group that would eventually swell to thirteen thousand. In the summer of 1942, Bob began to attract others, including an American civilian named Harry MacKenzie, a former mining superintendent on Luzon before the war.

MacKenzie brought Bob one of his most talented LGAF members—Juan Pajota, a brilliant young Filipino soldier who'd begun forming guerrilla squadrons himself in central Nueva Ecija, the Luzon province that includes the city of

Cabanatuan. After Bob and Juan met, Juan agreed to align his followers with LGAF. Bob also promoted him to captain. (These so-called "jungle promotions" were common in the guerrilla organizations, and leaders often promoted themselves too.)

Along with conducting raids on the Japanese, Bob Lapham's LGAF gathered intelligence and helped protect civilians from bandit gangs taking advantage of the chaos of war. It was a dangerous life. Bob's commander, Claude Thorp, who'd continued guerrilla activities after the Bataan surrender, was captured in the fall of 1942 and executed at Bilibid Prison in 1943.

Bob managed to avoid this fate. He was canny and adept at organization, and carefully planned escape routes from any camp or locale. Bob thought smaller, nimble groups of guerrilla fighters had a better chance of evading detection, so he developed a loose network of guerrilla units rather than one larger, centralized force.

Bob's LGAF wasn't the only guerrilla group operating behind enemy lines in the Philippines. Americans such as Bernard Anderson led another group, as did intelligence officer Russell Volckmann, who also had thousands of followers. Volckmann later used his guerrilla warfare experiences to help the army develop Special Forces units (sometimes known as Green Berets).

On Palawan Island, Nazario Mayor, active within the local Filipino guerrilla network there, helped care for several of the injured American POWs who escaped from the prison camp massacre, and coordinated their rescue with General MacArthur's headquarters in Australia by radio.

This communication was possible because MacArthur saw the value of guerrilla activity and had taken steps to encourage and support these fighters. For instance, MacArthur had arranged secret missions to the Philippines by submarine to provide the groups with training and radio trans- mitters. This enabled the guerrilla leaders to remain in close contact with his staff.

Captain Juan Pajota was an experienced soldier and guerrilla fighter who fought alongside Robert Lapham and played a key role in the liberation of Cabanatuan prison camp.

And while Bob's LGAF group conducted raids, Bob's highest priority was to gather intelligence—information that would be useful when the tide of war in the Pacific turned and American forces launched a campaign to retake the Philippines. LGAF collected information on Japanese troop strength, loca- tions, and activities—information that would help save the lives of American soldiers whenever they did return.

Once General MacArthur waded ashore on Leyte Island on October 20, 1944, Bob knew American landings on Luzon

Island would soon follow—and that increased his fears for the safety of the POWs at Cabanatuan. After all, the rumors of American landings had resulted in the murder of the prisoners on Palawan.

In the fall of 1944, Bob had urged his contacts at headquarters in Australia to allow his group to launch a rescue mission at Cabanatuan. "We wanted especially to make the attempt in late October or early November when we thought the Japanese would be preoccupied with resisting the Leyte landings, but all we could ever get was assurance that when landing began on Luzon, rescuing the prisoners would be given top priority.

"That never satisfied us, because we feared that once the Japanese thought such an invasion imminent, they would kill all the prisoners," Bob added. "Capt. Juan Pajota, one of my most imaginative and energetic officers, was as concerned about the matter as I was. We often discussed every imaginable aspect of a rescue operation."

As much as they wanted to forge ahead, the guerrilla fighters were realistic about the challenges. The total number of prisoners was unknown, as was their physical condition. Bob would have gladly welcomed fit fighters into his guerrilla units, but these POWs were likely to be in poor physical condition.

That presented a rescue challenge too. Evacuating hundreds of malnourished, ill men over rough terrain to the sea and trying to arrange transport by submarine or plane would be almost impossible.

"Whether there were 3,000 or the 'more than 500' that I estimated late in 1944, most of them would be weak, sick, and likely dispirited in the bargain," said Bob. "Even had they been willing to join our LGAF forces, they would have been not an asset but a heavy burden."

Bob and Juan Pajota had even discussed recruiting Filipino civilians to carry the prisoners to the sea to await evacuation. "Captains Pajota and Eduardo Joson [another effective guerrilla operative who postwar became the governor of Nueva Ecija province] assured me enthusiastically that they could find enough Filipino citizens to carry all the men, but even I was not optimistic enough to credit that," said Bob.

No, the rescue mission would have to wait—for now.

And as Bob Lapham counted down the days until the long-awaited return of American forces on Luzon, he could only hope they wouldn't be too late.

IN CAMP: LAST DAYS

EYEWITNESSES: RALPH HIBBS, HANK COWAN

All fall, Dr. Ralph Hibbs had watched anxiously as the guards began to choose prisoners to send to camps in Japan. In early December, the guards selected another group of POWs. This final exodus would leave only about five hundred men in camp.

The patients in his TB ward were passed over. This was a relief: Ralph didn't think these sick men would survive being taken to Japan. His turn came next. "Then all the medical officers, thirty-five in number, were lined up."

A Japanese lieutenant came down the line, pointing at each man and indicating whether he'd leave or stay. Ralph had once thought "survival was determined by guts, but now it was pure luck."

As the Japanese officer looked at him, Ralph realized the man recognized him as the TB doctor. The officer gave the order for Ralph to stay, one of only ten medical officers left. Ralph realized his fate might have just been decided—but what fate that might be he couldn't be sure. "This order might be a death sentence, since we were still convinced the few remaining prisoners would soon be liquidated."

Not long after, those fears seemed more real than ever when frightening reports reached the prisoners. "The grim news of a massacre at Palawan Island on 14 December, 1944, filtered in by bits and pieces . . . By late December the horrible event was confirmed," said Ralph. "This reinforced our fears that our camp would be liquidated."

Colonel Curtis Beecher, the highest-ranking American POW, had been moved out with the December exodus of prisoners. Many in this group were destined to die in the sinking of the hell ship *Oryoku Maru*. (Beecher survived and was liberated from a camp in Korea in September 1945.)

Beecher's absence meant that medical officer Colonel James W. Duckworth (nickname: "the Duck") was now the ranking officer for the POWs. Duckworth asked Ralph to be his adjutant, or assistant. Ralph's duties now included accompanying Duckworth to meetings with the Japanese camp commandant. The main message conveyed by the enemy in these meetings, Ralph soon found, was always the same. "'You must stay in the camp, work hard, give us no trouble, or you will be severely killed.'"

In October, the prisoners had heard rumors about American landings on Leyte Island. They could only wait to see when MacArthur would make good his promise to return to Luzon.

In early January, they heard gunfire in the north, in the direction of Lingayen Gulf. Ralph guessed what it meant:

American troops would be landing on Luzon within days. After months and years of waiting, the Americans, at last, had returned. Japanese forces in the Philippines were now on the defensive, just as the American and Filipino troops had been three years earlier.

"We could hear the rumble of big guns and the Japanese were moving men and equipment up the highway near our camp," Hank Cowan said. Hank, too, had been spared being transported on the ill-fated *Oryoku Maru*, and later told his daughter, Carolyn, that he was saved when a guard shoved him out of line and said, "You too sick!"

Hank noted, "There was intense air activity. Even at night, the planes would attack the Japanese transport trucks on the highway."

The military situation, both inside and outside the camp, was fluid and uncertain. The camp's guards disappeared, but the prisoners were ordered to stay in the camp or be killed. Later, other guards moved in, and groups of Japanese soldiers appeared and disappeared, sometimes stopping at the camp to rest.

Hank worried about these unknown enemy soldiers moving in and out of Cabanatuan. "They could come in and murder us at any time," he said.

Once, in mid-January, three tanks rolled into the camp and a Japanese lieutenant made signs that he was looking for a doctor. Ralph and a surgeon named Jim Musselman were called to examine a young Japanese soldier. Ralph guessed he was no more than eighteen and had suffered a severe head injury, apparently by falling off a tank. "Poor kid, a long ways from home, I thought."

The doctors found a long spinal needle and, with only candles for light, performed a procedure that confirmed a skull fracture. Using hand gestures, Ralph tried to convey to the Japanese tank officer that the young soldier's condition was extremely serious. The officer didn't understand and started to pick up the wounded man.

Ralph sprang forward and stepped between his patient and the enemy officer. "'No more riding on tank!' I shouted. 'Must not move!'"

All that night, Ralph and his colleague kept vigil beside their patient. By morning, the Japanese soldier was still alive, but had slipped into a deep coma. Even so, he was taken away and tied onto the tank, despite Ralph's protests. Ralph didn't believe his patient would survive for even a mile. "Although he was the enemy, the thought never entered my mind to do anything but to try to save the young soldier's life."

Confronting the tank officer had been incredibly dangerous. And had the enemy soldier died under the Americans' care, Ralph might have been beaten or even killed.

That wasn't the only disturbing incident the prisoners encountered. Another time, four soldiers with bayonets barged into the camp. It turned out they were searching for a certain guerrilla fighter. But these events worried Ralph.

As the chaos increased, it seemed possible to Ralph that any passing group of enemy soldiers might simply let loose and attack the POWs just "for kicks or for the Emperor . . . Our options were zilch. We waited with grim smiles on our faces. Tension mounted in the camp."

The Americans might be close, but the danger facing the prisoners at Cabanatuan seemed worse each day. Emaciated, exhausted, and sick, there was nothing Ralph or any of them could do.

"We were entirely defenseless," Ralph said.

THE RESCUERS: MAKING THE CASE

EYEWITNESSES: BOB LAPHAM, WALTER KRUEGER, HENRY MUCCI

On January 9, 1945, nearly a month after 139 POWs were murdered on Palawan Island, thousands of US troops came ashore at Lingayen Gulf on Luzon Island.

Not long after, guerrilla leaders including Bob Lapham, Bernard Anderson, and Russell Volckmann traveled to meet with General Walter Krueger, commander of the Sixth Army. It must have been an emotional meeting. After all, these three men had remained in enemy territory operating on their own with little contact with home for nearly three years—and against all odds they'd survived.

Now their groups were officially brought under Krueger's command; Filipinos who had been serving as guerrillas were incorporated into the Philippine Army.

Bob Lapham felt energized. At long last, help had arrived. "The thousands of us all over Luzon were now in the 'real' army and could fight alongside our fellows in a regular campaign to free the Philippines."

And that real army was impressive. Bob had spent years scrounging for supplies, equipment, and food. He was astonished at the force the United States was bringing to the fight. It was clear that much about the American war effort had changed since those discouraging months on Bataan back in 1942.

Filipino and American guerrilla fighters were instrumental in intelligence gathering prior to American landings on Luzon. This photo shows a group at General Krueger's headquarters at Calasiao in late January 1945. The original caption lists, from left to right, Lt. Hombre Bueno of the Philippine Army; Lt. William Farrell of Providence, RI; Major Robert Lapham (head of LGAF) of Davenport, IA; LT. James O. Johnson of Spencer, IA; Lt. Henry Baker and Lt. Gofronio Copcion of the Philippine Army.

For example, Bob was "utterly amazed . . . to see the thousands of troops supplemented by incredible quantities of U.S. weapons, supplies, and food that were unloaded from an armada of transports and stacked in veritable mountains on shore. Prominent amid this flood of materiel were innumerable tanks—and what tanks!

"They were not the puny 'tin cans' of 1941–42, armed with what now seemed like popguns, but thickly armed steel monsters bearing cannons that three years before had existed only in the field artillery. The spectacle not only bore no relationship to the Filipino world to which I had grown accustomed during the previous three years. It did not resemble anything I had ever seen in the prewar United States either."

Emerging from an isolated life undercover, Bob was witnessing for the first time the results of America's massive World War II production effort—an effort that had, of course, not come nearly in time to prevent the Philippines from falling to Japan.

"There is no question in my mind that the Allies won World War II by sheer numbers, amounts, quantities: more men, more guns, more money, more industry, more ships, more planes, more food," Bob marveled. "Most immediately, it was incontestable that the phantom 'reinforcements' awaited so impatiently ever since January 1942 had arrived at last—with a vengeance."

This changed everything. Now, Bob said, "Instead of trying to hide from the Japanese, we searched for them everywhere in the mountains and the plains."

As the Sixth Army established a beachhead and prepared to take on thousands of Japanese troops entrenched on Luzon, Bob's LGAF fighters accelerated their offensive actions, coordinating closely with the newly arrived American forces.

Bob explained, "We were at once set to patrolling, guarding ammunition and supply dumps, watching bridges and rear area installations, acting as scouts and guides, and clearing civilians out of the way of troops."

Later, Bob counted sixty-one actions by his LGAF guerrilla forces in the first month alone. From January 10 through February 10, the guerrillas ambushed trucks, sabotaged a bridge, and attacked Japanese patrols.

But one thing still weighed heavily on Bob Lapham's mind: Cabanatuan.

In late January, in the midst of this burst of activities, Bob Lapham rode a horse forty miles from Guimba to General Walter Krueger's Sixth Army Headquarters near Calasiao, just south of Lingayen Gulf.

Bob had moved his main camp to Guimba, which, like Cabanatuan, is in Nueva Ecija province. It was also the most forward point inland reached by American troops. Any rescue attempt of the POWs would be launched from here.

Since this was the front line of the advance, it also meant that once the prisoners were freed, they wouldn't be safe again until they reached Guimba. And between Guimba and Cabanatuan lay twenty-five miles of roads, rice paddies, and grasslands still controlled by Japan—enemy territory.

The rescue attempt posed incredible dangers to the weakened, malnourished prisoners. They'd have to walk or ride those twenty-five miles—and ideally move under the cover of darkness. How many prisoners were even able to walk? How many were dying because of the lack of medical treatment? No one knew.

A large-scale POW rescue like this, through so much enemy territory, had never been attempted. But in the evolving, dangerous military landscape, Bob didn't feel delay was possible. Cabanatuan might become another Palawan any day now.

This truly was a race against death.

Filipino guerrilla fighters and radio operators of the 978th Signal Service Company. The radio operators were dropped behind enemy lines a year before the US invasion to provide intelligence reports to General MacArthur.

Enlisted men's area at General Walter Krueger's Sixth Army Headquarters at Calasiao. Bob Lapham journeyed here to press for the Cabanatuan rescue mission to take place.

At headquarters, Bob first briefed General Walter Krueger's intelligence chief, Colonel Horton White. Bob explained that based on observations and intelligence gathered in the field, he now estimated that about five hundred prisoners remained in the camp—and, he emphasized, he had every reason to believe they were in serious danger.

Cabanatuan prison camp itself was smack in the middle of a massive movement of Japanese troops. It was also being used as a resting point as the Japanese forces moved north to prepare for a long siege. Groups of troops were stopping at the camp to rest for a night or a day. That meant there could be hundreds of enemy soldiers at the camp at any one time, making a rescue attempt more dangerous.

The presence of the Americans on Luzon added to the threats the POWs faced. After all, that is what had happened at Palawan—word of the arrival of Americans had led to murder of the POWs. A traditional attack, using tanks and large weapons, wouldn't work. If the Japanese got wind of the rescue in advance, the prisoners would likely be killed.

General Walter Krueger (seated) celebrated his sixty-fourth birthday on January 26, 1945. Born in Germany in 1881, he immigrated to the United States at the age of eight and enlisted in the army in 1899. He served in the Spanish-American War, the Philippine-American War, and World War I, rising throught the ranks. In World War II, he was asked by General MacArthur to take charge of the Sixth Army, leading combat operations in New Guinea as well as the Philippines.

General Krueger immediately grasped the urgency of the mission—and the need for speed, surprise, and secrecy. As soon as he was briefed, he authorized action to liberate the prisoners.

"Intelligence reports indicated that considerable enemy forces were being evacuated north through Cabanatuan," Krueger later wrote. "So it was obvious that any rescue attempt would have to be kept absolutely secret and preceded by a careful reconnaissance."

Timing would be crucial as far as when the raid took place, in order to avoid the scenario of a small number of rescuers facing an overwhelming number of Japanese troops billeted at the prison camp.

Another huge factor was the massive movement of Japanese troops now underway. Just as General MacArthur had confronted a superior, better-supplied Japanese force in 1941–1942, Tomoyuki Yamashita, the Japanese general now in charge of defending the Philippines, realized he couldn't hold on to all of Luzon against the Allies.

But Yamashita was also determined not to retreat to the malaria-ridden jungles of Bataan Peninsula as the Allies had done in late 1941; this would cut off his 275,000 troops from supplies and food sources, including access to rice and produce from farmlands.

Instead, Yamashita decided on a different strategy. Dividing his main forces on Luzon into three groups, he began moving them north of Manila to set up defensive positions in three cooler, mountainous areas that would still allow access to food supplies. His own group, called the Shobu, numbered more than 152,000 soldiers in January 1945. He chose as his headquarters the summer resort city of Baguio, about a hundred miles north of Cabanatuan.

Militarily, Yamashita's plan was sound. After the US had dropped atomic bombs on the cities of Nagasaki and Hiroshima, the Japanese emperor announced his nation's surrender to the Allies on August 15, 1945. Even then, Yamashita was still engaging Allied troops in northern Luzon; over a hundred thousand Japanese troops remained in the Philippines.

"Having decided to abandon the Central Plains-Manila Bay region, Yamashita concentrated his forces in three mountain strongholds that, he felt, the Allies could overrun only at the cost of many lives and much time," wrote one military historian.

As a result of the general's strategy, only minor delaying actions were taking place elsewhere on Luzon in late January. More importantly for planning the rescue attempt was the fact that many of the Japanese troops were using a highway that passed right by Cabanatuan—and with its capacity to hold a large number of soldiers, the prison camp made a convenient rest point.

"The Japanese had already evacuated many of the prisoners [at Cabanatuan], and Sixth Army Headquarters feared that they might move the remainder to the northeast or kill them to prevent their liberation," explained another historian.

"If these possibilities were to be averted, the Americans would first have to take the compound by surprise before their own main forces arrived in the area and then evacuate the prisoners to friendly lines before the Japanese could react."

General Krueger summed it up: "The success of the enterprise depended on secrecy and surprise. If the Japanese received any inkling of it they would probably massacre all the prisoners. Information of it was accordingly confined to very few persons, and coordination of effort was gained by briefing each member of the rescue force thoroughly on the plan as a whole on his own particular task."

Secrecy, stealth, speed, and surprise. That's what a raid would require—otherwise, men who had endured the hardship of fighting on Bataan, the Death March, Camp O'Donnell, and Cabanatuan, faced execution.

Success, then, depended on having accurate, up-to-date information about Japanese troops in the area in and around the camp; the prisoners needed to be rescued in a swift, nimble, hit-and-run operation; and the mission needed to include rear-guard defenses, to keep any enemy soldiers nearby from ambushing five hundred defenseless men and their small number of rescuers. Traveling for so long through the countryside also meant depending on the loyalty and cooperation of local citizens.

Luckily for POWs like Hank Cowan and Ralph Hibbs, General Krueger chose a leader who knew exactly how to accomplish all this. His name was Henry Mucci.

THE RESCUERS: A DARING PLAN

I t's time to meet Lieutenant Colonel Henry A. Mucci, General Krueger's choice to plan and lead the Cabanatuan rescue mission.

Mucci was a charismatic, no-nonsense West Point graduate and commander of the Sixth Ranger Battalion. He developed the plan with his chief aide, Captain Robert "Bob" Prince, along with Bob Lapham and three members of a specialized reconnaissance group called the Alamo Scouts: John Dove, Bill Nellist, and Tom Rounsaville.

They all shared one goal: to extricate the prisoners from inside Japanese territory without losing a single POW.

OVERALL RESCUE PLAN

Executing the rescue mission meant grappling with three main challenges:

1. **THE PRISON CAMP.** The prisoners must be liberated inside the camp quickly, which meant overwhelming the guards, finding the prisoners, and escorting them

out safely. That task would fall to about a hundred highly trained commando soldiers: members of the Sixth Rangers.

2. ENEMY TROOPS IN THE SURROUNDING AREAS. Reconnaissance in advance would determine the number and location of Japanese troops nearby. This would be done by two teams of Alamo Scouts with assistance from local guerrillas in advance of the mission. Once the raid began, gunshots would alert any enemy forces nearby. To protect the liberated prisoners as they set out, Filipino guerrilla fighters led by LGAF

Members of the Alamo Scouts played a key role in the Cabanatuan raid.

captains Juan Pajota and Eduardo Joson would serve as a rear guard, setting up roadblocks to engage and hold back any enemy that might be camped nearby or move in from nearby towns.

3. HELP FROM THE COMMUNITY. The prisoners would have to be brought safely through the night back to Guimba—a distance of twenty-five miles, not an easy trek through the countryside for sick and malnourished men. Juan Pajota proposed an innovative solution: recruiting civilians in the area to carry prisoners in their carabao carts. Along with benefiting men who might not be in any shape to walk, this method had the advantage of silence and stealth. The caravan could move easily through the back country rather than on dangerous roads.

CARRYING OUT THE PLAN:
ALAMO SCOUTS

The first part of the mission was entrusted to two teams of American soldiers called Alamo Scouts. Mucci's Rangers were trained for hand-to-hand combat and quick, nimble action; the Alamo Scouts were specialists in reconnaissance. Again, timing was crucial. The raid needed to take place within days, but at the best time to keep the POWs safe. To determine

Men of the Sixth Ranger Battalion. This photo was taken after the raid, with liberated prisoners in the background.

that, the rescuers required accurate, up-to-date intelligence about the strength of the Japanese troops around the prison camp. That's where the Alamo Scouts came in.

The Alamo Scouts were a small, specialized unit of only 138 men. The program had been launched in New Guinea by Major General Walter Krueger in late 1943. Before the end of the war, twelve small Alamo Scout teams conducted more than a hundred special missions behind enemy lines in the Pacific. (Note: The Alamo Scouts were a small American program, different than the prewar Philippine Scouts, which had trained Filipino soldiers like Juan Pajota.)

Two Alamo Scout teams led by William Nellist and Thomas Rounsaville were selected to take part in the Cabanatuan raid. Alamo Scout Lieutenant John Dove would travel with the Rangers and stay in radio contact with his fellow Scouts, serving as a liaison between the two groups.

The two Alamo Scout teams included Filipino Americans Thomas Siason, Sabas Asis, Rufo Vaguilar; Alfred Alfonso, a Hawai'i-born Filipino; and Francis H. LaQuier, a member of the Chippewa tribe from Minnesota. Of the 138 Alamo Scouts in World War II, records show that at least 15 were Native American.

Alamo Scout missions were top secret and remained classified until the 1980s. As a result, most of the Scouts received little recognition of their accomplishments at the time and for years after the war.

CARRYING OUT THE PLAN: RANGERS

Lieutenant Colonel Henry Mucci was in charge of the Sixth Ranger Battalion, a unit of nearly 600 men, and the brainchild of generals Douglas MacArthur and Walter Krueger.

Like the Alamo Scouts, the Rangers had undergone intensive, months-long training to give them the skills to conduct swift raids behind Japanese lines—including missions like the rescue at Cabanatuan. The Rangers would not rely on heavy equipment or artillery but on hand-to-hand combat skills and the ability to move quickly. Now they were about to undertake the mission for which they would go down in history: the greatest POW rescue of World War II.

Henry Mucci chose 120 men to participate in the raid; with officers, the Rangers' force totaled 128 men. It was a volunteer assignment, but there was no lack of soldiers eager to take part.

Captain Bob Prince was in command of Company C; First Lieutenant John F. Murphy headed Company F. The Rangers would travel light. Stealth was essential. The rescuers developed the plan quickly, but their preparations were thorough. In a later study of the rescue mission, combat operations analyst Dr. Michael King noted, "Mucci's men used aerial photographs in their planning, and every officer and enlisted man familiarized himself with the routes, rendezvous points, and the location of the objective."

CARRYING OUT THE PLAN: FILIPINO GUERRILLAS OF THE LGAF

In the end, Bob Lapham wasn't able to go on the mission himself. General Krueger believed Bob's knowledge about Japanese troops on Luzon made his participation too risky. Bob's talents would be needed as the Sixth Army prepared for the long fight ahead to win back Luzon.

However, Bob had full confidence in his captains, especially Juan Pajota, who knew the area well and had the trust of local citizens. Along with his key role during the rescue and the idea of using the water buffalo carts, Juan is credited with several other perceptive additions to the rescue plan. His years of guerrilla activity and his intimate knowledge of the region and its people proved invaluable.

For example, based on past observations of the Cabanatuan camp, Juan suggested flying a plane overhead to distract the guards just before the raid. Juan and his men also spread the word to encourage local people to pen chickens and bring dogs inside so they wouldn't make noise when rescuers, and later prisoners, too, traveled along the route to and from the camp.

Stealth was key to the first phase of the rescue, as Rangers entered the prison camp and attacked the guards. Once that happened, the noise of the guns *would* attract attention. This presented a special danger because of the camp's location on the Cabanatuan City–Cabu highway.

To prevent the prisoners from being attacked by any enemy troops in the area, the Filipino fighters would need to

197

block access. Juan Pajota's men would establish a roadblock at a bridge on the Cabu River, just a mile from the prison camp. The raid was scheduled to start at about 7:45 p.m. A time bomb would be set to explode fifteen minutes later so Japanese tanks and troops couldn't cross the bridge.

This task also fell to Captain Juan Pajota. Bob Lapham, for one, had absolutely no doubt he would pull it off.

As it turned out, there *were* many enemy soldiers in this area.

It also turned out that Juan was ready.

Filipino guerrilla fighters under the command of Captain Juan Pajota of the LGAF.

YOUR BRIEFING MAP

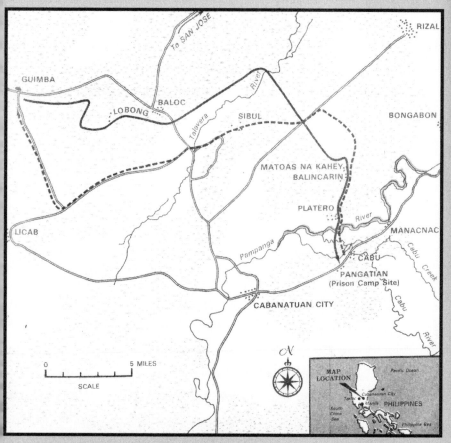

Please take a moment to look at this map, as it will help make clear what happened next. On this map, the prison camp is shown close to Pangatian. Can you find it? Next, note that the route taken by the rescuers from Guimba, to the east on the left side of the map, is shown in a solid line. Most of the terrain was open grasslands and rice paddies, making concealment difficult.

Eduardo Joson's guerrillas, shown by a cluster of dots, were stationed rather far along the road to Cabanatuan City to block any troops coming toward the camp from there. Juan Pajota's men, who engaged in the most intense fighting, were near Cabu, closer to the camp, shown by the dots that span the Cabu River. They were forced to engage with enemy troops billeted for the night in that area.

The escape route back to friendly territory in Guimba is shown with a dotted line.

CHAPTER 16

THE RESCUERS: ALL SYSTEMS GO!

When Henry Mucci called his Rangers together for a briefing before the rescue attempt, he requested that each participating soldier make a solemn pledge.

"I asked every man to swear he would die fighting rather than let any harm come to the prisoners of war under our care. I did that because I believed in it.

"Everybody on that mission took that oath."

After an intense but rapid planning process, it was time to put the plan into action. On the afternoon of Saturday, January 27, 1945, the two teams of Alamo Scouts left base camp in Calasiao, heading to Guimba. After nightfall, local Filipino guides accompanied them from Guimba to the village of Platero, about three miles north of the Cabanatuan prison camp.

At the village, with the help of local guerrillas, the Alamo Scouts gathered information about the number of guards at the camp, their routines, and the total of enemy troops billeted nearby.

The Rangers set out early the next day, Sunday, the twenty-eighth. They went by truck from base camp to Guimba, then left Guimba in the afternoon, marching east. They arrived at the town of Balincarin, near Platero, early on Monday morning, the twenty-ninth.

There, they met up with Alamo Scout leaders and Captain Juan Pajota. However, there were problems. The reconnaissance news wasn't reassuring. Large numbers of Japanese troops were bivouacked in the vicinity, and there was heavy traffic on the highway directly in front of the prison camp. The teams had also spotted several hundred enemy soldiers near Cabu Creek, just a mile north of the prison camp, and more in Cabanatuan City, a few miles south.

The raid had been planned for that night, but Lt. Col. Henry Mucci decided to delay for twenty-four hours, hoping the troop traffic on the road would lighten somewhat.

The raid was rescheduled for the evening of Tuesday, January 30.

The rescuers and the guerrillas took the extra time to finish preparations to convey the prisoners to safety. Juan Pajota and his men recruited two hundred volunteers willing to drive their carabao all night long and carry the liberated prisoners to Guimba. Arrangements were also made to feed up to 650 men on the return route. People living closest to the prison camp were advised to leave discreetly to protect their safety.

The night before the raid, the Rangers moved on to Platero, where residents treated them to a meal. All the maps, time frames, and aerial photographs were checked and rechecked.

After a nerve-biting delay of twenty-four hours, the latest reconnaissance showed that enemy traffic on the road was lighter. An estimated 73 guards were at the prison camp; about 150 others had stopped for the day there, apparently to rest. The prisoners were together in the northwest part of the compound. Nothing seemed out of the ordinary—so far, at least, the enemy had no idea what was about to happen.

There were still as many as eight hundred Japanese troops around Cabu. Even so, Mucci determined they couldn't wait any longer. Each man was briefed on his specific task.

January 30, 1945: All systems were go.

At 5:00 p.m., the Rangers headed for the prison camp.

Juan Pajota quietly moved his men, including about 90 armed and 160 unarmed, into position to form a roadblock on a highway bridge over Cabu River, three hundred yards northeast of the camp. Juan had something else up his sleeve, however. He'd sent ahead an additional 400 men (and four machine guns) to the Cabu area—just in case they were needed.

They would be.

Eduardo Joson's force of about 60 men positioned themselves south of the prison camp, to block any Japanese troops

Rangers crossing the Pampanga River on the afternoon of January 30, 1945, on the way to Cabanatuan, in advance of the 7:45 p.m. assault. The prisoners would need to recross the river after being liberated.

coming up from Cabu or Cabanatuan city. (Remember to go back and look at the map.)

At exactly 7:45 p.m., First Lieutenant John F. Murphy in Company F of the Rangers, positioned near the rear gate of Cabanatuan, shot off his rifle as a signal for the assault to begin. Company F focused on hand grenades and shooting at guard towers.

Meanwhile, Captain Bob Prince and the men of Company C had crawled through the grass the last mile to the main gate of

Rangers in tall grass en route to Cabanatuan prison camp on January 30, 1945. The grass closest to the camp was low, requiring the assault team to crawl so as not to be spotted by guards.

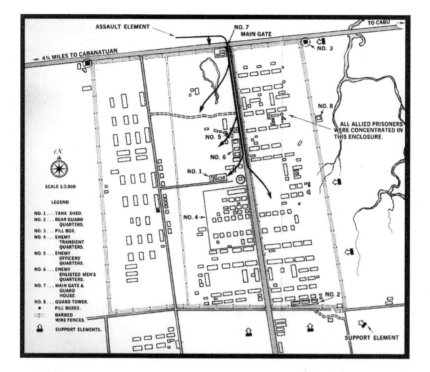

A diagram of the Cabanatuan prison camp showing the main gate and location of prisoners.

the camp. It took them seventy-five minutes. Once the firing from Company F began, the Rangers in Company C, on the opposite end of the compound, began firing at guard towers, shacks, and Japanese gun placements. The Rangers blasted the main gate open.

They couldn't know if the Japanese had any inkling of the raid and would be waiting for them. They couldn't know if they'd been betrayed. They stormed in anyway.

The Rangers took the enemy completely by surprise.

The force of the attack overwhelmed the guards; the enemy death toll was high. Within twelve minutes, Rangers were leading the first prisoners out. Two Rangers were killed in the rescue: Corporal Roy Sweezy and a physician, Captain James Canfield, son of author Dorothy Canfield Fisher.

Bob Prince conducted a search of the POW encampment before setting off a red flare to signal retreat. He missed one British man, Edwin Rose, who was deaf and had apparently fallen asleep near the latrines. He woke up the next morning to an empty camp but managed to find local guerrillas who escorted him to safety.

Meanwhile, on the bridge over the Cabu River, Juan Pajota's guerrillas engaged with a Japanese battalion camped only three hundred yards away. "The stunned Japanese counterattacked the Filipinos repeatedly in piecemeal fashion, suffering heavy casualties, but were unable to gain ground," wrote Dr. Michael King in his analysis. "Pajota also used a bomb to blow a gap in the bridge."

While Captain Joson's roadblock wasn't attacked, Juan and his men were still in the midst of fierce fighting when Bob Prince sent up his flare. The Filipino guerrillas, who had lost so many countrymen in the Bataan Death March and at Camp O'Donnell, fought until nearly 2:30 the next morning.

It was an incredible display of determination and grit. King summed it up: "His [Pajota's] guerrillas had virtually destroyed a Japanese battalion without suffering any fatalities."

IN CAMP: JUST BEFORE DARK

EYEWITNESSES: RALPH HIBBS, BOB PRINCE, HANK COWAN

Just before dark, a huge black plane, not over 200 meters up, swooped over the camp, soon followed by another fly over," said Dr. Ralph Hibbs on the evening of January 30.

Ralph wondered what it could mean. The plane's sudden appearance made him curious. He wandered over to the guard house, where he could see eight or ten men. All seemed quiet. "I watched for awhile and then strolled up the bare path and, with dark coming nearer, sat on the headquarters steps with my three good pals."

One of the men remarked that it seemed like something funny was going on. But what? Ralph and his friends had no way of knowing the plane was a diversionary tactic, the brainstorm of Captain Juan Pajota, who'd figured it would unsettle and distract the guards and keep them scanning the skies, rather than looking at the grass surrounding the camp as the Rangers approached as stealthily as they could.

Captain Bob Prince, who was in charge of leading Company C of the Sixth Rangers across the open landscape to the main gate, was thankful for the distraction. "This pilot came along and his instructions were to get over the prison camp and divert attention as we crawled across this field that probably seemed like half a mile but it was possibly closer to two or three hundred yards.

"By crawl you're on your belly and not on your knees and you had your rifle cradled across your elbows and you just sort of inched across this place," said Bob. "We knew he was above us and we could look up and see him, too. According to the prisoners we talked to later, he had everybody in the camp, American or Japanese, watching this pilot because he was just about five hundred feet elevation."

Once the Rangers had burst into Cabanatuan, some were deployed to shoot guards; others had one mission only: Get the prisoners out. But a few POWs were understandably confused by the unusual appearance of the Rangers, who wore fatigue uniforms with no insignias or rank.

The Rangers had also donned caps, rather than helmets, since helmets would have been bulkier and noisier. No wonder everyone wondered: *Who were these guys?*

Bob Prince recalled what happened when a private confronted Colonel James W. Duckworth, now the highest-ranking POW. "They [his men] had some arguments from the Colonel who was in charge of the prison camp," he said. "He was probably about a fifty-year old regular army doctor but he was the ranking man there.

"He [Duckworth] said we're not going anywhere without instructions from MacArthur. This private said, 'MacArthur says get your ass out of here, Colonel.'"

The first shots woke Hank Cowan. It took him awhile to figure out what was going on. "I had settled down for the night when all hell broke loose," recalled Hank.

"I was sure the Japanese were going to murder us. I jumped out of my bed and ran outside and started crawling toward the fence. I had only gone a few yards when I saw a big man in a strange uniform. My first thought was 'My God! Now the Germans are helping them!'"

Hank heard someone else ask the man if he was a Yank. "He said, 'Yes, let's get the hell out of here!'

"P.O.W.s were pouring out of the buildings," added Hank. "The word had spread fast and men that had been sick for months got up and walked out."

At 7:45 p.m., when a gunshot pierced the silence, Ralph Hibbs and his three friends were still sitting outside. Hearing the gunfire, one shouted, "'My God, they're finally going to kill us.'"

Shots were now blasting from the main guard house, where Ralph had just been. Seconds later, there seemed to be firing everywhere. Ralph and the others dove into the closest drainage ditch. Crouching, they saw explosions and fires in the Japanese headquarters. Enemy tanks and trucks burst into flames.

Then Ralph heard yelling from all over. "'We're the Yanks,' came the call. 'You're free. All Americans head for the main gate.'

"It was reported later one very proper Englishman among us said, 'I'm not an American, but I'm going too,'" Ralph said.

Ralph spied a soldier and clambered out of the ditch to ask what was going on. He got the same answer. "'We're the Rangers, you're free,'" he bellowed.

Still, Ralph persisted, unwilling to believe his own ears. Rangers? Who were the Rangers, anyway? Were they guerrillas? Where had they come from? But this Ranger had no time for questions. Ralph said, "The Ranger turned on me and yelled, 'Listen, you get the hell out of here. We're General Krueger's boys!'

"I pleaded, 'My men can't even walk.'

"'The rest of the prisoners have been carried out. You're the last damn one—now get going!'

"He picked me up with one hand and turned me downhill. Then he gave me a 'ten foot kick' squarely in the ass."

Ralph had to be sure. He wasn't about to leave without his patients in the TB ward. He fetched his first aid pack and then ran to the ward, sticking his head in the door and yelling. Silence. They were already gone!

Ralph was astonished. "My God, I thought, how did they do it?"

As he stumbled out to the main road, a Ranger urged him on, barking, "'You're the last man.'"

Ralph looked over his shoulder; there was a battle raging east toward Cabu, where Captain Juan Pajota's troops had established their roadblock. Ranger Bob Prince later remarked, "We couldn't have done it without the guerrillas. They protected our flank and then on the way back they formed our rear guard in case anybody should come after us."

Juan and his men weren't about to let up on that protection as the Rangers led the prisoners into the next dangerous phase of the rescue: the journey back to Guimba.

"In several ways the foremost hero in the operation was Capt. Juan Pajota. Before the actual attack he had managed to accumulate more men and four more machine guns than I knew we possessed," Bob Lapham said of his captain. "Immediately after the rescue Juan retreated in a direction designed to draw pursuers away from the liberated men.

"Incredibly, his unit did not suffer a single casualty, though scores or perhaps hundreds of the enemy were killed. This battle was Pajota's finest hour."

Accounts differ, but it seems likely that more than a thousand enemy soldiers were killed or wounded during the rescue, some inside the camp and others at Cabu. Ralph lost two of his TB patients who were already extremely ill; two Rangers were killed and several wounded. A number of Captain Juan Pajota's troops were injured but none killed. Many accounts record that 511 prisoners were rescued from the camp; 516 is the number used by the United States Army Office of the Command Historian.

THE ROAD BACK

EYEWITNESSES: HANK COWAN, RALPH HIBBS

Rangers escorting prisoners after the successful raid to free the camp.

e followed the Rangers out of camp across the rice fields toward the Pampanga River," said Hank Cowan. "A terrific battle was going on all around us and the bullets were buzzing by. We finally waded across the river and the shooting seemed to die down. I guess the Japanese decided not to follow us across the river."

A little while later, the column stopped and met up with the volunteer drivers, who loaded about five prisoners onto each carabao cart. "We still had a long way to go before we would be out of danger," said Hank.

"The Rangers were great. They gave their clothes and food to us without a second thought. In Platero, when a Filipino saw that I had no shoes, he took off his own and gave them to me. What a generous people they are."

As he left camp, Dr. Ralph Hibbs turned back to see flames leaping into the sky from the Japanese headquarters building.

Close-up of former prisoners as they journeyed to safety in the early morning hours of January 31, 1945.

"For the first time I was finally convinced that I was honest-to-God going to make it.

"Thank God for the safety of our little group. Guerrillas and civilians appearing out of the darkness guided me down the narrow trail."

Before long, Ralph stumbled into a man leaning against the dike of a rice paddy. It was Colonel James Duckworth, who'd fallen and broken his arm. "The bones grated as he moved but he refused anything for pain. I managed to make a sling with handkerchiefs and my precious socks," said Ralph. "Later this human bulldog, one tough cookie, was helped into a cart where he rode the rest of the night."

As the line inched forward in the darkness, local citizens along the path greeted the liberated prisoners, offered them food, and urged them on. "The column inched cross country, along the dikes, through the barrios [neighborhoods], and the groves of trees. People lined the trail offering bananas, mangoes and rice balls. The children would run up and touch us," Ralph said.

It was midnight when the column reached the main north-south highway heading toward Rizal. Discovery at this point would spell disaster, with the slow-moving men and carts unable to travel quickly. As a precaution, the Rangers set up roadblocks to the north and south. Luck was with them: The long line of liberated prisoners crossed safely.

At about 8:00 a.m. on the morning of January 31, the group stopped to rest at the small town of Sibul. Residents provided

Local citizens volunteered their water buffalo carts for prisoners unable to walk.

food and water and more carabao carts. At Sibul, Henry Mucci was able to establish radio contact with Guimba, and requested that trucks and ambulances meet the column, which set out again about 9:00 a.m.

"The trail lined with Filipinos was soon surrounded by U.S. tanks, armored cars and troop carriers, ambulances and a Red Cross van with food. All were filled with wildly cheering Americans. I never was certain which vehicle was the first to reach us, but I think the Red Cross van beat the tanks," said Ralph.

About two hours later, the group met the trucks and ambulances, which took the former prisoners to the 92nd Evacuation Hospital in Guimba. Ralph's joy was bittersweet.

Nearing Guimba, Carabao drivers who already unloaded prisoners too weak to walk line the road as other prisoners walk by.

Ambulances and trucks met the prisoners in the final stages of the journey to the evacuation hospital at Guimba.

A truckload of former POWs on the way to Guimba. The man standing at the left is General Richard Marshall, General MacArthur's chief of staff who evacuated to Australia with MacArthur from Corregidor in March 1942.

It had been heartbreaking to lose two patients, especially when they were so close to real medical help.

The mission was an unqualified success. It wasn't just the skill and bravery of the American soldiers. The rescue wouldn't have worked without the friendship and support of dedicated Filipino fighters and ordinary citizens. These were people who had endured years of hardships and terror under Japanese occupation, fought beside the Americans from the first day of the war, and lost tens of thousands of their own at Bataan and Camp O'Donnell. Still others had risked their lives as guerrillas and as activists in the Philippine underground.

Without the help of people living near Cabanatuan, who stepped forth to hold back the enemy, support the liberated prisoners, and help them reach safety, the greatest POW rescue of World War II might have had a tragic outcome.

Carlos Romulo put it this way, "They knew the land and its dangers. They knew the way it could be done."

THE FIRST TASTE OF FREEDOM

"American hamburgers were served to the men who could eat them. Nothing had ever tasted so good to me." —Hank Cowan

Thanks to combat photographers who accompanied the Rangers, photos of the historic Cabanatuan raid are now part of the National Archives.

While the rescue is less well-known today, it energized a war-weary nation eager for good news. Lieutenant Colonel Henry Mucci published an account of the rescue in the *Saturday Evening Post*, a popular magazine, in April 1945, making him a national hero.

Liberated Cabanatuan marines pose with Lt. Col Henry Mucci, seated third from the left.

Lt. Colonel Henry A. Mucci (left), commander of the Sixth Ranger Battalion, shakes hands with Colonel James W. Duckworth, senior officer among the liberated prisoners, who broke his arm in a fall during the escape. Dr. Ralph Hibbs assisted him in walking in the darkness until he was able to ride in a cart.

On the left, a Signal Corps photographer who accompanied the Rangers chats with a released prisoner. A photographer and a few soldiers returned to the prison camp to dig up hidden medical records, death logs, and buried camp literature, including the poems of Henry Lee, which found their way into Calvin Chunn's 1946 book *Of Rice and Men*, now rare and out of print.

Here, a prisoner is being interviewed on the radio. Liberated prisoners were greeted by radio and newspaper journalists eager to talk to share the incredible rescue with the world. The story of redemption and triumph electrified the American public.

A Ranger (left) chats with prisoners after their return to safety.

Clerks outside the hospital collect information from the released POWs so that cables could be sent to inform families back home that their loved ones were safe at last.

Newly released prisoners chat with local citizens.

Freed POWs rest on the porch of the hospital.

Wounded Rangers after the raid.

Liberated Cabanatuan POW Abie Abraham (right) stayed in the Philippines for more than two years after his release to help recover and identify the remains of Americans who died on the Bataan Death March. He was an avid speaker in schools and passed away in 2012 at the age of ninety-eight.

His obituary in the *Pittsburgh Post-Gazette* listed his long years of volunteer service. It also noted his advice. "'I always tell kids, 'When you meet a veteran, shake his hand and thank him for his sacrifice,'" Mr. Abraham told the *Post-Gazette* in 2005.

Abie Abraham is also featured in the permanent collection of the ADBC Museum (National American Defenders of Bataan and Corregidor) in Wellsburg, West Virginia. To learn more, visit the museum online at https://adbcmuseum.com/exhibits.

THE REAL HEROES

Eyewitnesses: Hank Cowan, Ralph Hibbs

W ith the swift rescue, many were stunned and bewildered," said Dr. Ralph Hibbs, looking back at that perilous night full of tension, fear, and hope. Guimba was a whirlwind. War correspondents and radio interviewers from around the world converged on the exhausted, dazed group. The men lined up to give their names so families back home could, at last, receive word they were alive.

The newly liberated POWs were brought to the 92nd evacuation hospital at Guimba, once a schoolhouse, where they were registered, evaluated physcially, and fed. Often these first meals made the malnourished men ill.

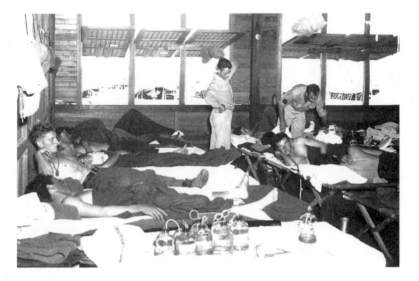

Liberated POWs in the hospital at Guimba.

Medical staff moved quickly to identify those in immediate need of attention. The sickest men were sorted. "IVs were started on others not responding well," said Ralph. "Hip bones stuck out. Spindly feet and legs, with bruised purple discoloration showed large chronic putrid ulcers."

Since he'd been serving as adjutant, Ralph gave many interviews along with Colonel James Duckworth. He was asked the same question again and again: How had they survived? How had they withstood so much suffering?

"'We're alive because of luck and the will to live,'" was the only answer he could think to give.

"Supposedly we were heroes since dead soldiers give poor interviews," he added. "There was never any doubt in my mind about that label. It belonged to those in graves in the jungle, to those buried on the Death March or at prison camps, not lucky bums like us."

At one point, Ralph was filled with unexpected emotion. "My heart stopped at the first sight of an American flag fluttering from the turret of a tank," he said. "What a sight, blurred through teary eyes."

A few days later, General Douglas MacArthur visited Colonel Duckworth in the hospital. Ralph was on a nearby cot and MacArthur sat next to him, across from "Duck." Ralph, then, became an eyewitness to an extraordinary encounter as the two men spoke for over an hour.

Colonel Duckworth described the deaths of senior officers MacArthur had known and the atrocities they had all endured. At one point, Ralph remembered, the general covered his face with his hands and cried.

"'I'm sorry it took so long,' he said in a deep husky whisper that was barely audible."

Ralph wrote later that he believed MacArthur's grief had been heartfelt and real. After all, MacArthur himself hadn't wanted to abandon the Philippines. The decision had been made by President Franklin D. Roosevelt, who'd had to prioritize scarce resources and help Great Britain and European allies fight Hitler.

Still. It had taken a long time. A very long time.

"There should be no cheering on our return, I thought, but a sober reflection on those heroes that lie in unmarked graves in the cane brakes," Ralph said. "The price of freedom comes

high—not only in lives but in suffering and those who mourn
their passing."

Ralph had lost friends and comrades, and he had lost Pilar.
Ralph never forgot this brave young woman. Long after the
war, in 1967, Ralph and his wife, Jeanne, visited the Philippines
to mark the twenty-fifth anniversary of the fall of Bataan. It
was then that Ralph determined to work for official recognition
of Pilar Campos and her brave efforts to help American POWs.

The process took until 1983. That year, Ralph returned
to the Philippines and located Pilar's surviving cousin,
who accepted a posthumous official citation of America's
appreciation.

"Friends have told me of the treatment of Pilar when she
was mortally wounded but I see her—standing tall at the door
of her home—her only weapon courage, her only defense
beauty and her life," he said. "Nothing more adds to the truth
of her passing."

Dr. Ralph Hibbs settled in Medford, Oregon, where he
practiced medicine and raised a family. He kept his pledge to
help others, and did international medical missions along with
serving patients in Oregon. After Jeanne's death, he married
again. Ralph wrote a memoir, *Tell MacArthur To Wait*, and
is also featured in *Ghost Soldiers* by Hampton Sides, a book
on the Cabanatuan rescue (see the bibliography for information on both titles.) He passed away in 2000 at the age of
eighty-seven.

Former POWs Pat Parker (left) and Hank Cowan (right) shortly after their liberation.

Like Ralph, Hank Cowan was overwhelmed with emotion when he first saw an American flag again. "I broke down and cried with joy."

The POWs healthy enough to leave the hospital in Guimba were sent closer to American forces. "At Lingayen a camp had been prepared for us," Hank said. He remembered that the former POWs ate twice the amount of rations as other soldiers. "A bond was forged between the prisoners and the Rangers and great friendships grew."

Hank continued, "We stayed at Lingayen for about a week, rested, ate good food, and gained weight. After a week, we boarded planes for Leyte. We were anxious to get home, but we did hate to leave our new friends. We stayed at Leyte for two days and boarded a transport ship for home.

"We made one stop in New Guinea. Our servicemen there gave us a tremendous welcome. We were given the run of the New Hollandia Army Base and could have anything we wanted. We stayed there only a few hours before resuming our trip to San Francisco and home."

Hank arrived in San Francisco on March 8, 1945. A few days later, former POWs healthy enough to do so attended a special celebration in their honor. They were welcomed to the city with a parade, with thousands cheering as they rode through the streets in Red Cross station wagons.

"We were taken to City Hall where Major [Bob] Lapham expressed the city's greetings and presented each of us with a medallion which had been struck as San Francisco's tribute to our heroism," Hank recalled. "Because we did not consider ourselves heroes we were overwhelmed by all the attention given to us, but we were thankful for it and will always remember the people of San Francisco.

"For me there will always be something special about the Golden City."

Special indeed. Hank's life was about to take an unexpected turn.

His daughter, Carolyn Mangler, one of Hank's three children, graciously shared this with me in an email: "My dad was one of the fortunate ones who was not sick enough to be confined to Letterman Hospital in San Francisco, so he was

Hank and Ginny Cowan wed on April 22, 1945, and were married for more than forty years.

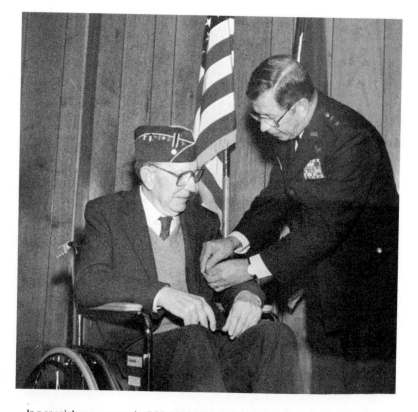

In a special ceremony on April 22, 1988 (his wedding anniversary), Hank Cowan, then suffering from prostate cancer, became the first recipient of the Prisoner of War Medal from the US Air Force, presented by Major General Lee V. Greer.

The Prisoner of War Medal was authorized by Congress to recognize the special service prisoners of war gave to their country and the suffering and anguish they endured while incarcerated.

hooked up with a couple of blind dates, the second one was my mom [Ginny]. This was just a few days after he got to San Francisco! Then he went to Roseville to visit his sister and told her he met his future wife.

"Dad came back to San Francisco and six weeks later they were married. I can't imagine how fast it was! Dad passed from prostate cancer in 1988, and my mom died almost to the day 5 years later. I persuaded my mom and dad that they should have a big celebration for their 40th anniversary and I'm glad I did because they didn't make it to the 50th."

Hank worked at McClellan Air Force Base in Sacramento, California, as a carpenter until he retired, and died on November 29, 1988.

Hank couldn't know you would be reading about his wartime experiences so many years later. But, thanks to his children, his remarkable story was preserved. When I began researching this book I was lucky enough to find his story online in a post dated May 1, 1972, thirty years after he survived the Bataan Death March.

At the beginning of his memoir, Hank wrote, "The men in my story were once young and full of life. Now they are nothing but faded heroes, remembered by a few aging buddies.

"What I have endured I would gladly endure again if it would help my country. I pray that we will never again endure another Pearl Harbor or Bataan.

"Please let others read this story lest we forget."

And now you have done just that. Remember them.

OUR SMALL
WHITE CROSSES

Survivors of the Bataan Death March remember their fallen comrades.

World War II veterans tear up during an emotional speech at the Seventy-Fourth Bataan Day Anniversary—Capas Shrine, Tarlac, Philippines in April 2016.

"Group Four"
Cabanatuan Concentration Camp Cemetery
by Lt. Henry G. Lee

We'll have our small white crosses by and by,
Our cool green lawns, our well-spaced,
well-cared trees,
Our antique cannons' muzzled to the sky,
Our statues and our flowers
and our wreaths.
We'll have our bold-faced bronze
and copper plaques
To tell in stirring words of what we saved

Troops gather to witness the historic signing of surrender papers on the USS *Missouri*, September 2, 1945.

And who we were, with names and dates;
our stacks
Of silent rifles, spaced between the graves.
We'll have our dedication by and by
With orators and bands to set us free—
And shining, well-fed troops. Above will fly
The planes with stars we never lived to see.
We'll have our country's praises here below.
They'll make a shrine of this small bit of Hell
For wide-eyed tourists; and so few will know
And those who know will be the last to tell
The wordless suffering of our lives of slaves,
Our squalid deaths beneath this dripping sky,
The stinking tangle off our common graves.
We'll have our small white crosses by and by.

PEACE BE NOW RESTORED

Sailors, photographers, and journalists from around the world gathered for the signing of the official Japanese surrender papers on the USS *Missouri* in the American-occupied port of Yokohama, Japan, on September 2, 1945.

General Douglas MacArthur and his party stayed at the New Grand Hotel in downtown Yokohama, where he was reunited with General Jonathan Wainwright, who had been liberated from a prison camp in Manchuria after being transferred there from the Philippines.

This never-before-seen-photograph of the surrender signing on the USS *Missouri* was taken at 9:05 a.m. on September 2, 1945, by Staff Sergeant Jake Churchman, a member of General Douglas MacArthur's communication unit. Although he was ordered to stay on another ship, Churchman went on board the *Missouri* that morning and snapped this shot of the proceedings from where he sat. Jake Churchman donated his photo collection to the National American Defenders of Bataan and Corregidor Museum. The museum and Carol Chapman have graciously allowed this photo to be published for the first time.

Ninety-seven-year-old Bataan survivor Ben Skardon at the Bataan Memorial Death March in 2015. He began participating in the annual march in 2007. Ben died on November 15, 2021, at the age of 104, just days after learning of his honorary promotion to brigadier general. A 1938 graduate of Clemson University, he credited two fellow alumni with keeping him alive in Bataan. He later taught at Clemson and inspired members of the Clemson University community to take part in the march.

Detail of a bronze memorial entitled "Heroes of Bataan," created by artist Kelley S. Hestir for Veterans Park in Las Cruces, New Mexico. At the base surrounding the statue are footprints: impressions made from survivors and symbolizing those who suffered and died on the Bataan Death March. About eighteen hundred men from New Mexico fought in the Philippines; fewer than nine hundred made it home.

MacArthur spoke briefly before the papers were signed by Japan, the United States, and other Allied nations. When all the representatives had signed, MacArthur spoke again.

"'Let us pray that peace be now restored to the world and that God will preserve it always. These proceedings are closed.'"

TIMELINE OF MAJOR EVENTS OF WORLD WAR II IN THE PACIFIC

1941

DECEMBER 7 — Japanese attack Pearl Harbor; Japan launches attacks in Hong Kong, Siam, Malaya, Guam, and the Philippines.

DECEMBER 8 — President Roosevelt asks Congress to declare war on Japan, launching the United States into World War II. In the Philippines, Clark Field is attacked.

DECEMBER 9–10 — Japan attacks Nichols Field and Cavite Naval Base, dismantling American air and sea power in the Philippines.

DECEMBER 22 — Japanese land invasion of the Philippines begins.

DECEMBER 24 — General Douglas MacArthur moves his army headquarters from Manila to the island of Corregidor, "the Rock"; American and Filipino troops retreat to Bataan.

DECEMBER 26 — Manila is declared an open city to avoid destruction and civilian casualties.

1942

JANUARY 2 — Japanese forces enter the city of Manila, Philippines.

MARCH 11 — General MacArthur is evacuated to Australia on the order of President Franklin D. Roosevelt.

APRIL 9 — General Edward "Ned" King surrenders Luzon forces on Bataan, and the Bataan Death March begins.

MAY 6 — General Jonathan Wainwright surrenders Corregidor.

JUNE 9 — Remaining Allied forces in the Philippines surrender, giving General Masaharu Homma a delayed victory.

1943

FEBRUARY 9 — Americans claim victory on Guadalcanal.

MARCH 2 — Japanese troop ships incur heavy losses in Battle of the Bismarck Sea, in the South West Pacific.

AUGUST — US and Allied forces adopt "leapfrogging" attack strategy across Pacific islands, including the Gilbert and Marshall Islands, with the goal of reaching and invading Japan.

1944

JANUARY 29– FEBRUARY 7 — US forces drive the Japanese from the Marshall Islands, securing Majuro on January 31 and Kwajalein atoll by February 7.

FEBRUARY 23–JUNE — US begins operations in the Marianas, which include Saipan and Guam.

FEBRUARY 29 — US lands troops to begin takeover of Admiralty Islands.

APRIL–JULY — General MacArthur completes takeover of New Guinea.

JUNE 15 — US forces land on Saipan in the Marianas, securing it within three weeks.

JULY 21 — US forces land on the island of Guam.

OCTOBER 20 — General MacArthur's Sixth Army lands at Leyte, beginning fulfillment of his pledge to return and liberate the Philippines from Japanese occupation.

OCTOBER 23–26 — Battle of Leyte Gulf in the Philippines, in which the US Navy defeats the Japanese Navy, demolishing much of the enemy's remaining power at sea.

OCTOBER 26– DECEMBER 25 — Leyte Gulf is secured, bringing the end of the war closer.

1945

JANUARY 9 — General Douglas MacArthur leads US troops onto the beach on Luzon.

FEBRUARY–JUNE — American troops reach Manila in early February; a fierce battle takes place in the city, which is liberated by early March. By February 26, the US has recaptured Corregidor, "the Rock." Efforts to fully liberate Luzon and clear Manila Harbor of mines continue until the end of June.

MARCH — In attempts to force the Japanese government to surrender, the US begins B-29 bombing raids against major Japanese cities, including Tokyo, Kobe, Osaka, and Yokohama, killing thousands of civilians.

APRIL 1 — US forces invade the island of Okinawa, Japan.

APRIL 12 — President Franklin D. Roosevelt dies.

MAY 8 — Germany surrenders, ending World War II in Europe.

AUGUST 6 — The US drops the first atom bomb, on Hiroshima, Japan.

AUGUST 9 — The US drops a second atom bomb, on Nagasaki, Japan.

AUGUST 14 — Japan accepts surrender on August 14 and Emperor Hirohito announces it to his nation on August 15.

SEPTEMBER 2 — Surrender documents are signed between Japan and the Allies aboard the USS *Missouri*, officially ending World War II.

RESOURCES TO EXPLORE

Here are links to museums, articles, and oral histories to continue your learning journey. These links are current at the time of this writing, but please note that websites change often, so if you are unable to connect, try to search by the subject matter. Remember, when searching for fact-based information, it's always a good idea to start with museums, historical societies, and research libraries.

MORE ON CABANATUAN

Cabanatuan POW Camp, Philippines
http://www.mansell.com/pow_resources/camplists/
philippines/Cabanatuan/cabanatuan_main.html

Office of the Command Historian: Rescue at Cabanatuan
https://arsof-history.org/articles/v14n2_cabanatuan_
endnotes.html

PRISONERS OF WAR

Japanese Hell Ships
https://www.history.navy.mil/browse-by-topic/wars-conflicts-
and-operations/world-war-ii/1944/oryoku-maru.html

MacArthur Memorial, Ben Steele POW Art Exhibit
http://www.macarthurmemorial.org/435/Ben-Steele-POW-Exhibit

National POW Museum
https://www.nps.gov/ande/planyourvisit/natl_pow_museum.htm

PBS, *American Experience*: "The Bataan POWs"
https://www.pbs.org/wgbh/americanexperience/features/
bataan-pows/

PBS, *American Experience*: "Japan, POWS, and the Geneva Conventions"
https://www.pbs.org/wgbh/americanexperience/features/
bataan-japan-pows-and-geneva-conventions/

GENERAL WORLD WAR II

The 93rd Infantry Division: The African American Soldiers in the Pacific
https://warfarehistorynetwork.com/2019/01/19/the-93rd-
infantry-division-the-african-american-soldiers-in-the-pacific/

African Americans in the Navy: World War II, Naval History & Heritage Command
https://www.history.navy.mil/content/history/nhhc/
our-collections/photography/people-special-topics/
african-americans-in-the-navy/african-americans-and-the-
navy-wwii.html

National Park Service, "Latinos in World War II: Fighting on Two Fronts, Proving Valor in War, Seeking Equality at Home," by Lorena Oropeza
https://www.nps.gov/articles/latinoww2.htm.

Oregon Secretary of State, Life on the Home Front, "A Mixed Reception: Japanese Americans Return to Oregon"
https://sos.oregon.gov/archives/exhibits/ww2/Pages/after-
back.aspx

Native American Alamo Scouts: "Remembering the Alamo Scouts: Many American Indians Fought in World War II"
https://indiancountrytoday.com/archive/remembering-the-
alamo-scouts-many-american-indians-fought-in-world-war-ii

Pearl Harbor National Memorial
https://www.nps.gov/perl/index.htm

USS *Bowfin* Submarine Museum and Park
https://www.bowfin.org

VETERANS' ORAL HISTORIES & ARTICLES

Lorenzo Banegas
Video Interview, Library of Congress https://memory.loc.gov/
diglib/vhp/story/loc.natlib.afc2001001.87863/mv0001001.
stream

Lorenzo Banegas: University of Texas at Austin
https://voces.lib.utexas.edu/collections/stories/lorenzo-banegas

Ruben Flores
https://www.angelfire.com/nm/bcmfofnm/names/names_pu/
rubenflores.html

Sam Grashio
A video of Sam describing his rescue by the submarine USS
Bowfin: https://www.youtube.com/watch?v=cHYFrLfkDNU.

Bob Lapham
Profile from Office of the Command Historian
https://arsof-history.org/articles/v14n2_cabanatuan_sb_
lapham.html

THE BATAAN DEATH MARCH & WWII IN THE PHILIPPINES

Angels of Bataan—Nurse POWs, National WWII Museum
https://www.nationalww2museum.org/war/articles/nurse-pows-bataan-and-corregidor

Atomic Heritage Foundation: World War II and New Mexico
https://www.atomicheritage.org/history/world-war-ii-and-new-mexico

PBS, *American Experience*: "Bataan Death March"
https://www.pbs.org/wgbh/americanexperience/features/bataan-masaharu-homma-and-japanese-atrocities/

Bataan Memorial, Las Cruces, NM
https://www.lascrucescvb.org/bataan-memorial-2/

Bataan Project
https://bataanproject.com/

Filipino Veterans Fighting for Benefits
https://www.history.com/news/filipino-americans-veterans-day

Liberating the Philippines, 1945
https://www.nationalww2museum.org/war/articles/liberation-of-philippines-cecilia-gaerlan

National American Defenders of Bataan & Corregidor (ADBC) Museum, Education, and Research Center (ADBC Museum)
https://adbcmuseum.com/

New Mexico National Guard/200th Coast Artillery
https://www.angelfire.com/nm/bcmfofnm/history/briefhistory.html

New Mexico History Museum: 200th Coast Artillery
https://www.nmhistorymuseum.org/exhibition/details/2312/
before-bataan-new-mexicos-200th-coast-artillery

PBS, *American Experience*: "Juan Pajota"
https://www.pbs.org/wgbh/americanexperience/features/
bataan-juan-pajota-and-filipino-contributions-raid/

Philippine Scouts Heritage Society
https://www.philippinescouts.org/

Santo Tomas Internment Camp
https://cnac.org/emilscott/santotomas01.htm

"The Day We Cried: Hundreds of New Mexicans Endure Bataan Death March"
https://www.santafenewmexican.com/news/local_news/
the-day-we-cried-hundreds-of-new-mexicans-endure-
bataan-death-march/article_9f850acf-3ae0-5d8a-809a-
e00105de5217.html

USS *Trout* **and Rescue of the Philippine Gold**
http://www.navsource.org/archives/08/08202.htm

BIBLIOGRAPHY

BOOKS

Alexander, Larry. *Shadows in the Jungle: The Alamo Scouts Behind Japanese Lines in World War II*. New York: NAL Caliber, 2010.

Bank, Bert. *Back from the Living Dead: The Bataan Death March, 33 Months in a Japanese Prison and Liberation by the Rangers*. Middletown, DE: Major Bert Bank, 2019. Originally published in 1945.

Batcheler, John F., and Shelly E. McCandliss. *Cabanatuan: A Prisoner's Perspective*. Shelly E. McCandliss, 2018.

Beck, John Jacob. Foreword by Clare Booth Luce. *MacArthur and Wainwright: Sacrifice of the Philippines*. Albuquerque: University of New Mexico Press, 1974.

Binkowski, Edna Bautista. *Code Name: High Pockets: True Story of Claire Phillips, an American Mata Hari, and the WWII Resistance Movement in the Philippines*. Limay, Philippines: Valour Press, 2006.

Bocksel, Arnold A. *Rice, Men and Barbed Wire*. Hauppauge, NY: Michael B. Glass & Assoc., 1991.

Breuer, William B. *The Great Raid on Cabanatuan: Rescuing the Doomed Ghosts of Bataan and Corregidor*. New York: John Wiley & Sons, Inc., 1994.

Bumgarner, John R., M.D., *Parade of the Dead: A U.S. Army Physician's Memoir of Imprisonment by the Japanese, 1942–1945*. Jefferson, NC: McFarland & Company, Inc., 1995.

Cannon, M. Hamlin. *Leyte: The Return to the Philippines.* The War in the Pacific series. Washington, DC: Center of Military History, United States Army, 1993.

Chunn, Calvin E., ed. *Of Rice and Men: The Story of Americans Under the Rising Sun.* Los Angeles: Veterans' Publishing Company, 1946.

Cowan, James H. "Barbed Wire and Rice," Wagner High Online Alumni, https://whoa.org/publications/stories/barbedwire/.

Dyess, Lt. Col. William E. *Bataan Death March: A Survivor's Account.* Lincoln, NE: University of Nebraska Press, 2002. Originally published in 1944.

Fessler, Diane Burke. *No Time for Fear: Voices of American Military Nurses in World War II.* East Lansing, MI: Michigan State University Press, 1996.

Glusman, John A. *Conduct Under Fire: Four American Doctors and Their Fight for Life as Prisoners of the Japanese, 1941–1945.* New York: Viking, 2005.

Grashio, Samuel C., and Bernard Norling. *Return to Freedom.* Tulsa, OK: MCN Press, 1982.

Hibbs, Ralph Emerson. *Tell MacArthur To Wait.* New York: Carlton Press, 1988.

Huff, Col. Sid, with Joe Alex Morris. *My Fifteen Years with General MacArthur.* New York: Paperback Library, Inc., 1964.

Johnson, Forrest Bryant. *Hour of Redemption: The Heroic WWII Saga of America's Most Daring POW Rescue.* New York: Warner Books, 2002.

Jopling, Lucy Wilson. *Warrior in White.* San Antonio, TX: The Watercress Press, 1990.

Kaminski, Theresa. *Angels of the Underground: The American Women who Resisted the Japanese in the Philippines in World War II*. New York: Oxford University Press, 2016.

Keith, Bill. *Days of Anguish, Days of Hope*. Longview, TX: Stonegate Publishing, 2011.

King, Michael J. *Rangers: Selected Combat Operations in World War II*. Fort Leavenworth, KS: Combat Studies Institute, 1985.

Krueger, General Walter. *From Down Under to Nippon: The Story of Sixth Army in World War II*. Nashville, TN: Battery Press, 1989.

Lapham, Robert, and Bernard Norling. *Lapham's Raiders: Guerrillas in the Philippines 1942–1945*. Lexington, KY: The University Press of Kentucky, 1996.

Lascher, Bill. *Eve of a Hundred Midnights: The Star-Crossed Love Story of Two WWII Correspondents and Their Epic Escape across the Pacific*. New York: William Morrow, 2016.

Lawton, Manny. *Some Survived: An Eyewitness Account of the Bataan Death March and the Men Who Lived Through It*. Chapel Hill, NC: Algonquin Books, 2004.

Marston, Daniel, ed. *The Pacific War: From Pearl Harbor to Hiroshima*. Oxford: Osprey Publishing, 2005.

McManus, John C. *Fire and Fortitude: The US Army in the Pacific War, 1941–1943*. New York: Caliber, 2019.

Monahan, Evelyn M., and Rosemary Neidel-Greenlee. *And If I Perish: Frontline U.S. Army Nurses in World War II*. New York: Anchor Books, 2003.

Moore, Stephen L. *As Good as Dead: The Daring Escape of American POWs From a Japanese Death Camp.* New York: Caliber, 2016.

Morton, Louis. *The Fall of the Philippines.* The War in the Pacific series. Washington, DC: Center of Military History, United States Army, 1993.

Mydans, Carl. *More than Meets the Eye.* New York: Harper & Brothers, 1959.

Norman, Elizabeth M. *We Band of Angels: The Untold Story of the American Women Trapped on Bataan.* New York: Random House, 2013.

Norman, Michael, and Elizabeth M. Norman. *Tears in the Darkness: The Story of the Bataan Death March and Its Aftermath.* New York: Picador, 2009.

Phillips, Claire "High Pockets," and Myron B. Goldsmith. *Manila Espionage.* Los Angeles: Enhanced Media, 2017.

Reynolds, Bob. *Of Rice and Men: From Bataan to V-J Day, A Survivor's Story.* Monee, IL: Mindanao Books, 2019.

Romulo, Carlos P. *I Saw the Fall of the Philippines.* Garden City, NY: Doubleday, Doran & Co., 1943.

____.*I See the Philippines Rise.* Garden City, NY: Doubleday & Company, Inc., 1946.

Rottman, Gordon L. *The Cabanatuan Prison Raid: The Philippines 1945.* New York: Osprey, 2009.

Sides, Hampton. *Ghost Soldiers: The Epic Account of World War II's Greatest Rescue Mission.* New York: Anchor, 2001.

Sloan, Bill. *Undefeated: America's Heroic Fight for Bataan and Corregidor.* New York: Simon & Schuster, 2012.

Smith, Robert Ross. *The Approach to the Philippines*. The
War in the Pacific series. Washington, DC: Office of the
Chief of Military History, Department of the Army, 1953.

____. *Triumph in the Philippines*. The War in the Pacific
series. Washington, DC: Center of Military History,
United States Army, 1991.

Toll, Ian W. *Twilight of the Gods: War in the Western
Pacific, 1944–1945*. New York: W. W. Norton &
Company, 2020.

Utinsky, Margaret. *Miss U: Angel of the Underground*. San
Antonio, TX: Naylor, 1948. Reprint, 2017.

Volckmann, R. W. *We Remained: Three Years Behind
the Enemy Lines in the Philippines*. New York: W. W.
Norton & Company, 1954.

Weinstein, Alfred A., M.D. *Barbed Wire Surgeon: A Prisoner
of War in Japan*. Atlanta: Deeds Publishing, 2014.
Originally published in 1948.

Wilbanks, Bob. *Last Man Out: Glenn McDole, USMC,
Survivor of the Palawan Massacre in World War II*.
Jefferson, NC: McFarland & Company, 2004.

Willoughby, Amea. With the assistance of Lenore Sorsby.
*I Was on Corregidor: Experiences of an American
Official's Wife in the War-torn Philippines*. New York:
Harper & Brothers, 1943.

Wright, John M., Jr. *Captured on Corregidor: Diary of
an American P.O.W. in World War II*. Jefferson, NY:
McFarland & Company, 2009. First published in 1988.

Zedric, Lance Q. *Silent Warriors of World War II: The
Alamo Scouts Behind Japanese Lines*. Ventura, CA:
Pathfinder Publishing of California, 1995.

REPORTS, ARTICLES, INTERVIEWS, AND WEBSITES

ABQJournal.com. "Obituary for Flores." April 17, 2002._ http://obits.abqjournal.com/obits/print_obit/110571.

Atomic Heritage Foundation. "Bataan Death March." https://www.atomicheritage.org/history/bataan-death-march.

Bataan-Corregidor Memorial Foundation of New Mexico, Inc. "A Brief History of the 200th and 515th Coast Artillery." https://www.angelfire.com/nm/bcmfofnm/history/briefhistory.html.

____. "Bataan was the scene of many atrocities." March 29, 1999. https://www.angelfire.com/nm/bcmfofnm/names/names_pu/rubenflores.html.

____. "Survivor went from small-town life to face the ravages of war." Originally from *Las Cruces Sun News,* https://www.angelfire.com/nm/bcmfofnm/themen/lorenzobanegas.html.

Bataan Project. https://bataanproject.com.

Divine Word Missionary Seminary. "Fr. Theodore Buttenbruch, SVD (1886–1944)." https://sites.google.com/dwms.ph.education/dwms/about/fr-theodore-buttenbruch.

Erickson, James W. "*Oryoku Maru* Roster." https://www.west-point.org/family/japanese-pow/EricksonCSV.htm.

Gaerlan, Cecilia. "Liberation of the Philippines 1945." National World War II Museum. September 1, 2020. https://www.nationalww2museum.org/war/articles/liberation-of-philippines-cecilia-gaerlan.

Guise, Kim. "'To Sustain, not Destroy': Operation Swift Mercy and POW Supply." National WWII Museum.

September 18, 2020. https://www.nationalww2museum.
org/war/articles/operation-swift-mercy-and-pow-supply.

Harris, Heather, and Lisa Beckinbaugh. "Historical Report:
U.S. Casualties and Burials at Cabanatuan POW Camp
#1." Department of Defense, Defense POW/MIA Agency.
https://www.dpaa.mil/Portals/85/Documents/Reports/
U.S.Casualties_Burials_Cabanatuan_POWCamp1
.pdf?ver=2017-05-08-162357-013.

Mucci, Henry A. "We Swore We'd Die or Do it!" *The
Saturday Evening Post*, April 1945.

_____ "Rescue at Cabanatuan," *Infantry Journal*, April 1945.

National Museum of the Pacific War. "Robert Prince Oral
History Interview." September 17, 2004, https://
digitalarchive.pacificwarmuseum.org/digital/collection/
p16769coll1/id/9084/.

New Mexico History Museum. "Before Bataan: New
Mexico's 200th Coast Artillery." https://www
.nmhistorymuseum.org/exhibition/details/2312/
before-bataan-new-mexicos-200th-coast-artillery.

PBS. *American Experience*. "Japan, POWS and the
Geneva Conventions." https://www.pbs.org/
wgbh/americanexperience/features/bataan
-japan-pows-and-geneva-conventions/.

Schaarsmith, Amy McConnell. "Abie Abraham /
Survivor of Bataan Death March, volunteer at
VA hospital," *Pittsburgh Post-Gazette*, March
24, 2012. https://www.post-gazette.com/news/
obituaries/2012/03/24/Abie-Abraham-Survivor-
of-Bataan-Death-March-volunteer-at-VA-hospital/
stories/201203240157.

Schurtz, Christopher. "A Man's Song of Life and Death," *Las Cruces Sun News*, April 12, 2002, The University of Texas at Austin Voces Oral History Center, "Lorenzo Banegas." https://voces.lib.utexas.edu/collections/stories/lorenzo-banegas.

Tirado, Michelle. "Remembering the Alamo Scouts: Many American Indians Fought in World War II." Indian Country Today. Updated September 13, 2018. https://indiancountrytoday.com/archive/remembering-the-alamo-scouts-many-american-indians-fought-in-world-war-ii.

Veterans History Project, American Folklife Center, Library of Congress. "Lorenzo Y. Banegas Collection." (AFC/2001/001/87863). https://memory.loc.gov/diglib/vhp/bib/loc.natlib.afc2001001.87863.

____. "Ruben Flores Collection." (AFC/2001/001/87862). https://memory.loc.gov/diglib/vhp/bib/loc.natlib.afc2001001.87862.

SOURCE NOTES

The following pages tell you where to find the sources of the quotations in this book. A quotation enclosed in double quotation marks (like this ". . .") means the quoted words are from a direct or primary source, perhaps a book, an interview, or a war patrol report. When you see single marks inside double quotation marks ("' . . . '"), that indicates a quotation or dialogue that appears within a source.

EPITAPH

"Please let . . . ": James H. Cowan, "Barbed Wire and Rice," Wagner High Online Alumni, https://whoa.org/publications/stories/barbedwire/, 1.

"The bravest are usually . . . ": F Sionel José, *Dusk: A Novel* (New York: The Modern Library, 1984), 236.

BUZZING ENGINES IN THE SKY

"I had been working . . .": Cowan, 2.

Hank's family: Email from daughter Carolyn Mangler to author, 9/8/2021.

"some of the finest . . . ": Cowan, 1.

"I looked up . . . ": ibid., 2.

PART 1: FROM SHOCK TO SURRENDER

"To the Congress of the United States . . . ": Day of Infamy Speech by Franklin D. Roosevelt, December 8, 1941; SEN 77A-H1, Records of the United States Senate; Record Group 46; National Archives.

"The military unpreparedness. . . .": Lapham and Norling, *Lapham's Raiders*, xi.

CHAPTER 1: THE FIRST DAYS: HORROR AND DESTRUCTION

Japanese pilots' surprise: Morton, *Fall of the Philippines,* 90.

"I snuggled as close...": Cowan, 2–3.

"A burst of 20 mm fire . . .": ibid., 3.

"As the bombers passed over . . .": Morton, 86.

"The Japanese did a thorough job . . .": Cowan, 3.

Destruction at Clark: Morton, 88.

"the only way . . .": Grashio and Norling, *Return to Freedom*, 1.

"I thought of flying . . .": ibid.

"Ed took the bet . . .": ibid., 2.

"was the most inspiring . . .": ibid., 6.

"no doubt that . . .": Dyess, *Bataan Death March*, 24.

"We turned back . . .": Grashio and Norling, 4.

"I veered sharply . . .": ibid., 5.

"The wind shrieked . . .": ibid.

"I had barely gotten . . .": Jopling, *Warrior in White*, 35.

"I kept looking . . .": ibid.

"I had a ward full . . .": ibid.

Pilar Campos bio: Facebook, "Encyclopedia Olongapo" [city in Philippines], https://www.facebook.com/tgkbgapo/posts/1746079672301161/.

"'If I had to do it . . .'": Hibbs, *Tell MacArthur To Wait,* 17.

"A sinking feeling . . .": ibid., 21.

"The shrieking crescendo . . .": ibid., 28.

"Damn it, in my panic . . .": ibid.

"Nichols Field was in shambles . . .": ibid., 29.

"The whole of my life . . .": Willoughby, *I Was on Corregidor*, 75.

"heavy masses of earth . . .": ibid., 82–83.

"It was sickening . . .": ibid., 84.

"Everywhere the Allies . . .": Grashio and Norling, 9.

Advance landings: Morton, 98–99.

MacArthur rank: ibid., 17.

"shorts, short-sleeved shirt . . .": ibid., 29.

Reinforcements: ibid., 31-32.

CHAPTER TWO: RETREAT! GET OUT!

"It was the day before . . .": Willoughby, 96.

"Trussed up . . .": ibid., 101.

"It seemed unlikely . . .": ibid., 100.

"We had nothing to eat . . .": Jopling, 36.

"The seat came . . .": ibid.

"'Don't get mixed up . . .'": Hibbs, 42.

"I learned to work . . .": Romulo. *I Saw the Fall of the Philippines*, 47.

"'I'll be back, Carlos!'": ibid., 62.

"Christmas Eve— . . .": ibid., 63.

"Early in the morning . . .": Mydans, *More than Meets the Eye*, 68.

"It was late in the day . . .": ibid., 71.

CHAPTER THREE: STAYING ALIVE ON BATAAN

Hospital #2: Norman, *We Band of Angels*, 39–43.

"Sometimes when bombs and shells landed . . .": Jopling, 38.

"We would see . . .": ibid.

"We only ate . . .": ibid.

"Eating everything we could . . .": ibid., 39.

"The average diet . . .": ibid.

"'At first the food . . .'": Bataan-Corregidor Memorial Foundation of New Mexico, Inc., "Bataan was the scene of many atrocities."

"The quartermaster . . .": Veterans History Project, "Ruben Flores Collection."

"Mentally, it was devastating . . .": ibid.

"By the end of March . . .": Jopling, 40.

"We never had . . .": Hibbs, 57.

"The fighting was intense . . .": ibid.

"done nothing except . . .": ibid., 47.

"We made judgment calls . . .": ibid., 57–58.

"In January it averaged . . .": ibid., 85.

"I felt weak . . .": ibid., 106.

"Later that very . . .": ibid., 107.

"I wore it till . . .": Jopling, 40.

"By April, hunger and disease . . .": ibid., 41–42.

"Walking out . . .": ibid., 42.

"An earthquake shook . . .": ibid., 43.

"This was the day . . .": Jopling, 43.

"'We are not surrendering . . .,": "Ruben Flores Collection."

"'Captain, you will begin . . .'": Beck, MacArthur and Wainwright, 175.

CHAPTER FOUR: CORREGIDOR: IN THE TUNNEL

Corregidor: Beck, MacArthur and Wainwright, 39.

"Life in the Malinta Tunnel . . .": Jopling, 44.

"Heat and the odor . . .": ibid., 44–45.

"a giant anthill . . .": Willoughby, 109.

"There wasn't enough . . .": Romulo, *I Saw the Fall of the Philippines*, 104.

"on my next visit . . .": ibid., 132–133.

"A nurse's work . . .": Willoughby, 146.

"The ambulances raced . . .": Romulo, *I Saw the Fall of the Philippines*, 123–124.

"The first time . . .": Willoughby, 163.

"'Say, lady . . .'": ibid.

"Once I even beat . . .": ibid., 164.

"Our main talk . . .": Romulo, *I Saw the Fall of the Philippines*, 129.

"What Sutherland had to tell me . . .": ibid., 219.

"shouting in a voice . . .": ibid., 132–133.

"But the carrying . . .": ibid., 225.

"I said, 'I'll stay . . .'": ibid.

"'It was ordering . . .'": Beck, 123.

"'*I came through* . . .'": Beck, 168.

USS *Trout*: http://www.navsource.org/archives/08/08202.htm.
"The bars were brought . . .": Willoughby, 196.
"For three hours . . .": ibid., 197–198.
"He remembered how hard . . .": ibid., 199.
"Our instructions were . . .": ibid., 205.
"I stood there . . .": ibid., 233.
"As soon as we landed . . .": 245–246.
"Mind you, they said . . .": ibid., 247.
"The memory of Corregidor . . .": ibid.
"'You are not forgotten . . .'": ibid.
"Of course there couldn't be . . .": ibid., 182.
"We were impressed . . .": ibid., 138.

CHAPTER FIVE: SURRENDER: FIRST BATAAN, THEN CORREGIDOR

Troop numbers are estimates due to the confusion at surrender and the subsequent loss of
 life on the Death March: Sloan, *Undefeated: America's Heroic Fight for Bataan and
 Corregidor*, 183; Gaerlan, "Liberation of the Philippines 1945."
"There was no doubt . . .": Cowan, 6.
"By March 1942 . . .": ibid., 9.
"We walked all night . . .": ibid.
"It seemed like . . .": ibid.
"the Pacific Fleet . . .": Morton, 583.
"The battle for Bataan . . .ibid., 467.
"We're the Battling . . .": Atomic Heritage Foundation, "Bataan Death March." The limer-
 ick is credited to journalist Frank Hewlett.
"had earned the right . . .": ibid.
Romulo title: Romulo, *I Saw the Fall of the Philippines*, 241.
"Everyone in the place . . .": ibid., 247.
"'Bataan is hopeless.'": ibid., 272.
"I was the last man . . .": ibid., 1.
"'You're under orders . . .'": ibid., 275.
"The little launch . . .": ibid., 276–277.
"Hundreds of bombs . . .": ibid.
"The Japanese artillery . . .": ibid., 282-283.
"It was the funniest . . .": ibid., 289.
"The Old Duck creaked . . .": ibid., 293.
"'Bataan has fallen . . .'": ibid., 302.
"And we didn't . . .": ibid.
Japan military plans: Morton, 56–57.
"The beach defenses . . .": ibid., 536.
"I was so sick . . .": Jopling, 45.
"'Get up and get out . . .'": ibid., 47.
"Soon the world . . .": ibid.

Nurse POWS: Kim Guise, "Nurse POWs: Angels of Bataan and Corregidor,"
National WWII Museum. https://www.nationalww2museum.org/war/articles/
nurse-pows-bataan-and-corregidor.

"War is Hell . . .": Jopling, 129.

"'With profound regret . . .'": Morton, 561.

"By noon on 6th May . . .": Hibbs, 123.

"We surrendered only . . .": Grashio and Norling, 27.

PART 2: ENDURANCE AND RESISTANCE

"'*Gone are the hopes . . .*'": Hubbard in Chunn, *Of Rice and Men*, 217.

CHAPTER SIX: THE BATAAN DEATH MARCH

"I had taken my rifle . . .": Cowan, 10.

"We were held in this open . . .": ibid.

"The Battle of Bataan . . .": ibid.

"As we walked . . .": ibid.

"They marched us without . . .": ibid.

"The heat was terrible . . .": ibid.

Distances of Death March: McManus, *Fire and Fortitude*, 135.

"The Bataan Death March . . .": Falk, S., in Dyess, *Bataan Death March*, xi.

Tsuji: Glusman, *Conduct Under Fire*, 162–163.

Bataan Death March statistics: Harris and Beckinbaugh, "Department of Defense Historical Report, U.S. Casualties and Burials," 1–3.

"At 3 a.m. of April 12, 1942 . . .": ibid., 84.

"The March was a macabre . . .": ibid., 37.

"He then gave Ed . . .": Grashio and Norling, 38.

"As we departed . . ." Cowan, 11.

"*So you are dead . . .*": Lee, in Chunn, 204.

CHAPTER SEVEN: CAMP O'DONNELL: DEATH AT THE END OF THE MARCH

"There was no room . . .": Dyess, 94.

"The atmosphere was foul . . .": ibid., 94–95.

"My broken tooth . . .": Grashio and Norling, 44.

"Later I heard . . .": Dyess, 95.

"As we straggled on . . .": ibid., 97.

"But some were overlooked . . .": ibid.

"I saw a forbidding maze . . .": ibid.

"When we had been . . .": ibid., 101.

"flies by the millions . . .": ibid., 101–102.

"Mosquitoes descended . . .": ibid., 102.

"It may seem . . .": ibid., 111.

Prisoner's death toll estimate: Breuer, *The Great Raid on Cabanatuan*, 59–60.

O'Donnell statistics: Harris and Beckinbaugh, 3.

30 percent: "The March and Imprisonment at Camp O'Donnell," Britannica, https://www.britannica.com/event/Bataan-Death-March/ The-march-and-imprisonment-at-Camp-ODonnell.

"The buildings were soon . . .": Cowan, 11.

"was designed to slowly starve . . .": ibid., 12.

"God only knows . . .": Cowan, 13.

"I saw the trees . . .": ibid., 13.

Andersonville of the Pacific: John C. McManus, "Andersonville of the Pacific," Humanities, National Endowment for the Humanities, https://www.neh.gov/article/ andersonville-pacific.

"In other camps . . .": Mydens, 184–185.

Cabanatuan camp: Harris and Beckinbaugh, 4.

CHAPTER EIGHT: FROM CAMP O'DONNELL TO CABANATUAN

"Any place, we thought . . ." Dyess, 120.

"As we passed . . .": ibid., 121.

"We didn't care . . .": ibid.

"We probably wouldn't . . .": ibid.

"Prisoners from Bataan . . .": ibid., 122.

"goose size . . .": Hibbs, 165–166.

Gillespie: "Gillespie, PFC James W.," Bataan Project, https://bataanproject.com/ provisional-tank-group/gillespie-pfc-james-w/.

Beecher: "Beecher, Lt. Col. Curtis T.," Bataan Project, https://bataanproject.com/ proviso-students/beecher-lt-col-curtis-t/.

"I found out later . . .": ibid., 13–14.

"living skeletons . . .": ibid., 13.

"This must have saved . . .": ibid.

"Someone brought me . . .": ibid.

"The burying detail . . .": ibid.

"'The diphtheria caused . . .'": Bataan-Corregidor Memorial Foundation of New Mexico, "Survivor went from small-town life to face ravages of war."

"'They called it . . .'": ibid.

New Mexico death toll: New Mexico History Museum, "Before Bataan: New Mexico's 200th Coast Artillery."

"'Ruben Flores and I . . .'": Schurtz, "A Man's Song of Life and Death."

Smithsonian: "Survivor went from small-town life to face ravages of war."

CHAPTER NINE: CABANATUAN: RATS, RICE, AND LICE

"The main activity . . .": Grashio and Norling, 57.

"The basic trouble . . .": ibid.

Sam Grashio on faith: ibid., 75.
"It was a diet . . .": ibid., 56.
"Anything that ran . . .": ibid., 57.
"'I didn't catch . . .'": Chunn, *Of Rice and Men*, 34–35.
"At first I wanted . . .": Dyess, 106.
"It was in fairly large . . .": ibid., 123.
"There was hardly . . .": ibid.
"We used it . . .": ibid.
"Charcoal was salvaged . . .": Cowan, 14.
"Obtain from the black market . . .": Dyess, 123.
"The rice drew flies . . .": ibid., 124.
"I didn't want to go . . .": ibid., 148.
"So many men died . . . ": Cowan, 14.
"What a relief . . . ": ibid.
"I acquired a large pair . . . ": ibid.
"When we first came . . . ": ibid., 15.
"More than 27,465 . . . ": Guise, "'To Sustain, Not Destroy': Operation Swift Mercy and POW Supply."
"That Japanese forces . . . ": PBS, *American Experience*, "Japan, POWs, and the Geneva Conventions."
"Beatings became . . . ": Cowan, 15.
"In a prison camp . . . ": ibid., 16.
"Mail was distributed . . . ": Hibbs, 194.
"a truly remarkable sight . . . ": ibid., 165.
"'MacArthur just rolled up . . .'": ibid., 191.
"Red in the Eastern sun . . .": Lee, in Chunn, 211–12.
"'The best I can say . . .'": ibid., 184.

CHAPTER TEN: RALPH AND PILAR: BILIBID TO CABANATUAN

"They put troops . . .": Hibbs, 124.
"They allowed us . . .": ibid., 125.
"There was a certain relief . . .": ibid.
"'Don't get mixed up . . .'": ibid., 42.
"The Filipinos, as a people . . .": Romulo, *I See the Philippines Rise*, 38.
"My assigned space . . .": Hibbs, 127.
"It was amazing . . .": ibid.
"'Ralph, Pilar asked . . .'": ibid., 132.
"The next day . . .": ibid.
"I felt warm inside . . .": ibid., 133.
"'I'll try to see you . . .'": ibid.
"The first time . . .": ibid., 137.
Pilar's bravery: ibid., 136.
"'I'd rather stay here . . .'": ibid., 140.

"Our next stop . . .": ibid., 141.

"Guard towers manned . . .": ibid., 145–146.

"Their only crime . . .": ibid., 147.

Neary is listed on several rosters tracking POWS including that compiled by James S. Erickson, https://www.west-point.org/family/japanese-pow/EricksonCSV.htm.

"Prison life for a medical . . .": Hibbs, 160.

"Everything happening . . .": ibid.

"Those walking . . .": ibid.

"On several mornings . . .": ibid., 150.

"Agonizing abdominal cramps . . .": ibid., 155.

"It saved the camp . . .": ibid., 156.

"The tuberculosis ward . . .": ibid., 173–174.

Medical procedures: ibid., 178.

"I looked up . . .": ibid, 189.

PART 3: RACE AGAINST DEATH

"Surrounding our troopship . . .": Romulo, *I See the Philippines Rise*, 3–5.

CHAPTER ELEVEN: FALL 1944: NEW HOPES, NEW FEARS

"Late in 1944 . . .": Cowan, 19.

"This camp was like . . ." Hibbs, 181.

"The moment I saw . . . ": Cowan, 19.

"A huge roar . . .": Hibbs, 200.

"The sound of the guns . . .": Cowan, 19–20.

"After this first . . .": Hibbs, 200.

Prisoner exodus: ibid., 202.

"Hundreds of my best friends . . .": ibid.

"I wondered what . . .": ibid.

CHAPTER TWELVE: POWS IN DANGER

"Hollywood-style cowboy . . .": Lapham and Norling, *Lapham's Raiders*, 173.

The plight of the prisoners . . .": ibid., 176–177.

"Training or no . . .": ibid., 26–27.

Thorp capture: ibid., 48–50.

"We wanted especially . . .": ibid., 177.

"That never satisfied . . .": ibid.

"Whether there were 3,000 . . .": ibid., 178.

"Captains Pajota . . .": ibid., 178–181.

CHAPTER THIRTEEN: IN CAMP: LAST DAYS

"Then all the medical . . .": Hibbs, 204.
"survival was determined . . .": ibid., 203.
"This order might be . . .": ibid., 204.
"The grim news . . .": ibid., 205.
"'You must stay . . .'": ibid., 206.
Hank Cowan and guard: Email correspondence from Carolyn Mangler to author, 8/19/2021.
"We could hear . . .": Cowan, 20.
"They could come in . . .": ibid.
"Poor kid, a long ways . . .": Hibbs, 210.
"'No more riding on tank . . .'": ibid.
"Although he was . . .": ibid., 211.
"for kicks or for the Emperor . . .": ibid.
"We were entirely . . .": ibid.

CHAPTER FOURTEEN: THE RESCUERS: MAKING THE CASE

"The thousands of us . . .": Lapham and Norling, 175.
"utterly amazed . . .": ibid., 173–174.
"There is no question . . .": ibid., 174.
"Instead of trying to hide . . .": ibid., 176.
"We were at once . . .": ibid., 175.
"Intelligence reports indicated . . .": Krueger, *From Down Under to Nippon*, 237.
General Yamashita: Smith, *Triumph in the Philippines*, 95, 652.
"Having decided to abandon . . .": ibid., 94.
"The Japanese had already . . .": King, *Rangers: Selected Combat Operations in World War II*, 56–57.
"The success of the enterprise . . .": Krueger, 238.

CHAPTER FIFTEEN: THE RESCUERS: A DARING PLAN

Native American Alamo Scouts: Tirado, "Remembering the Alamo Scouts: Many Native Americans Fought in World War II."
Alamo Scouts: Alexander, *Shadows in the Jungle*, 5.
"Mucci's men . . .": King, 57.

265

CHAPTER SIXTEEN: THE RESCUERS: ALL SYSTEMS GO!

"I asked every man . . .": Mucci, "We Swore We'd Die or Do it!"
"The stunned Japanese . . .": ibid., 66.
"His [Pajota's] guerrillas . . .": ibid., 69.

CHAPTER SEVENTEEN: IN CAMP: JUST BEFORE DARK

"Just before dark . . .": Hibbs, 212.
"I watched for awhile . . .": ibid., 213.
"This pilot . . .": National Museum of the Pacific War, "Robert Prince Oral History Interview."
"They [his men] had some arguments . . .": ibid., 9.
"I had settled down . . .": Cowan, 20.
"I was sure . . .": ibid.
"He said . . .": ibid.
"'My God, they're. . . .'": Hibbs, 213.
"'We're the Yanks . . .'": ibid., 214.
"'We're the Rangers . . .'": ibid.
"The Ranger turned on me . . .": ibid.
"My God, I thought . . .": ibid.
"'You're the last man . . .'": ibid.
"We couldn't have done it . . .": Prince, 10.
"In several ways . . .": Lapham and Norling, 180–181.

CHAPTER EIGHTEEN: THE ROAD BACK

"We followed the rangers . . .": Cowan, 20.
"We still had . . .": ibid., 20–21.
"For the first time . . .": Hibbs, 216.
"The bones grated . . .": ibid.
"The column inched . . .": ibid., 218.
"The trail lined . . .": ibid., 221.
"They knew the land . . .": Romulo, *I See the Philippines Rise*, 213.
"American hamburgers . . .": Cowan, 21.
"I always tell kids . . .'": Schaarsmith, "Abie Abrahan / Survivor of Bataan Death March."

CHAPTER NINETEEN: THE REAL HEROES

"With the swift rescue . . .": Hibbs, 222.
"IVs were started . . .": ibid.

"'We're alive . . .'": ibid.

"Supposedly we were heroes . . .": ibid., 224.

"My heart stopped . . .": ibid., 223.

"'I'm sorry it took . . .'": ibid., 227.

"There should be . . .": ibid., 241.

"Friends have told me . . .": ibid., 249.

"I broke down and cried . . .": Cowan, 21.

"At Lingayen . . .": ibid., 21.

"We stayed at Lingayen . . .": ibid.

"We were taken . . .": ibid., 22.

"My dad was . . .": Mangler, Email to author, September 13, 2021.

"The men in my story . . . ": Cowan, 1.

EPILOGUE: OUR SMALL WHITE CROSSES

We'll have our small . . . : Lee, in Chunn, 219–220.

MacArthur and Wainwright: Toll, *Twilight of the Gods*, 754–755.

"'Let us pray . . .'": ibid., 761.

New Mexico National Guard casualties: Bataan Corregidor Memorial Foundation of New Mexico, Inc., "A Brief History of the 200th and 515th Coast Artillery."

PHOTOGRAPH AND ILLUSTRATION CREDITS

Photos ©: Alamy Images: 238 bottom (M L Pearson), 234 (Nathan Allen), 173 (PJF Military Collection), 233 (ZUMA Press Inc); American Defenders of Bataan and Corregidor Museum: 237; Combat Studies Institute, U.S. Army Command and General Staff College: 199, 205; Courtesy of the Cowan family: 5 left, 230, 231; Eastern Oregon University: 156, 157; Getty Images: cover (Daxus); The family of Daniel and Lucy Jopling: 10, 80, 81; Library of Congress: iv, 45, 66, 88, 93, 95, 100; National Archives and Records Administration: xi, xxx–1, 2, 5 right, 19, 23, 25, 32, 33, 39, 40, 41, 43, 51 left, 51 right, 68, 70, 82 bottom, 84, 86, 87, 90, 92, 98, 105, 109, 113, 115 top, 115 bottom, 117, 125, 127, 131, 135, 141, 142, 145, 148, 158–159, 162, 167, 170, 182, 185, 186, 187, 194, 198, 203, 204, 212, 213, 215, 216 top, 216 bottom, 217, 218, 219 top, 219 bottom, 220 top, 220 bottom, 221 top, 221 bottom, 222 top, 222 bottom, 223, 224, 225, 228, 235; New Mexico History Museum: 122 (Edward Vindinghoff/Courtesy Palace of the Governors Photo Archives); Naval History and Heritage Command: 15, 17, 49, 82 top; Shutterstock: cover, 29 (Carl Mydans/The LIFE Picture Collection); Tom Kelley: 11; US Air Force: 8, 13; US Army: 4 (Center of Military History), 6, 16 (Center of Military History), 26 (Center of Military History), 192, 238 top (Sgt. Marcus Fichtl, 24th Press Camp).

INDEX

Page numbers in *italics* refer to illustrations.

271

ACKNOWLEDGMENTS

Books about history are books about people and their experiences. *Race Against Death* wouldn't exist without the courage of veterans who shared their stories, and the families of former POWs who graciously allowed us to use family photographs to help bring these stories to life.

I'm most grateful to Carolyn Mangler, daughter of Hank Cowan, for her generosity in sharing information, anecdotes, and photographs. I'd also like to thank the families of Dr. Ralph Hibbs and Dan and Lucy Wilson Jopling for their assistance.

Thanks also to historian Michael Edwards and Jim Brockman, director of the National American Defenders of Bataan and Corregidor Museum. Both gave so generously of their time to read the manuscript and offer suggestions for improvement. Any remaining errors are mine.

People often say that writing is a solitary experience. In my experience, nothing could be further from the truth. In addition to the firsthand accounts of people who lived these events and the scholarship of historians, writers like me rely on a dynamic, creative team to bring books to readers. I am so fortunate to have an extraordinary editor in Lisa Sandell, who continues to inspire me with her compassion and dedication. I'd also like to thank my wonderful agent, Steven Malk, for all his help over the years.

Many of the people who make books like this have jobs that may be unfamiliar to readers. A special note of gratitude goes out to Cian O'Day, who went above and beyond the call to track down many hard-to-find photos for this book, a task made especially challenging since most of the photo research took place in 2020 and 2021, when the coronavirus pandemic closed a number of museums, libraries, and archives.

Thanks also to the entire Scholastic team who work to encourage reading and especially books like this that explore lesser-known aspects of history. Thank you to Lori Benton, Ellie Berger, Rachel Feld, Lisa Broderick, Lizette Serrano, Emily Heddleson, Kelli Boyer, Laura Beets and the entire Book Fairs team, Stephanie Yang, David Levithan, Amy Bradford, Mindy Stockfield, Emily Teresa, Arianna Arroyo, and many others. This book owes much to many talented professionals, including copyeditor Erica Ferguson. Thank you!

I wish to thank educators, teachers, librarians, and parents for encouraging young people to read nonfiction—and to write. Thanks also to friends and family for your support. I'm writing your names in alphabetical order and hope I don't forget anyone: Maya Abels and Stewart Holmes; Deniz Conger; Janice Fairbrother; Vicki Hemphill and Steve Johnston, along with Keelia, Meghan, and Aili and their amazing loved ones; Kristin Hill and Bill Carrick, Candace Fleming, C. Howard, Bonnie Johnson, Elisa Johnston, Fiona Kenshole, Katie Morrison, Sheridan Mosher, Rosanne Parry, Emily Picha, Kiara Sausedo, Judy Sierra, Becky and Greg Smith, Ellie Thomas, Vickie Tino, Teresa Vast and Michael Kieran, and my across-the-country workmates, the talented Deborah Wiles and incomparable Jim Pearce.

To Andy, Dimitri, Rebekah, Eric, and Oliver—I love you more than words can say. Finally, writing *Race Against Death* has brought back loving memories of my dad, Russell, who served in the Pacific; my mom, Gloria, also joined up during World War II. Like many of the veterans in this book, they returned to marry and raise a family.

They served and made sacrifices to fight authoritarianism and dictatorial rule, and make a stand against persecution and the violation of human rights. The freedoms they fought for were not, and are still not, enjoyed by all Americans and people around the world. Nor can we ever take democracy for granted.

Yet that hope for what America could be sustained POWs like Hank Cowan and Ralph Hibbs through their long ordeal. Seeing the American flag again brought tears to their eyes. I think that's worth remembering as we take up the challenges of our own time.

ABOUT THE AUTHOR

Deborah Hopkinson is the author of picture books, middle grade fiction, and narrative nonfiction for young readers. Her book *Titanic: Voices from the Disaster* won a Robert F. Sibert Honor. Her recent titles include *We Must Not Forget: Holocaust Stories of Survival and Resistance*, named an Orbis Pictus Recommended Book; *We Had to Be Brave: Escaping the Nazis on the Kindertransport*, a Sydney Taylor Notable Book; the Deadliest series, including *The Deadliest Diseases Then and Now*, *The Deadliest Hurricanes Then and Now*, both selections of the Junior Library Guild, and *The Deadliest Fires Then and Now*; and *D-Day: The World War II Invasion That Changed History*; among many others. Deborah lives in Oregon. Follow her on Twitter: @deborahhopkinson and Instagram: @deborah_hopkinson.